LOOK TWICE

YOUR GUIDE TO STAYING SAFE IN AN UNSAFE WORLD

VOLUME I

TIM BEARD

**Look Twice: Your Guide to Staying Safe
in an Unsafe World, Volume I**
Copyright © 2025 Tim Beard

Produced and printed by Stillwater River Publications.
All rights reserved. Written and produced in the United States
of America. This book may not be reproduced or sold in any
form without the expressed, written permission
of the author and publisher.

Visit our website at
www.StillwaterPress.com
for more information.

First Stillwater River Publications Edition.

ISBN: 978-1-965733-61-5

Library of Congress Control Number: 2025907442

1 2 3 4 5 6 7 8 9 10
Written by Tim Beard.
Interior photographs provided by Tim Beard.
Cover & interior book design by Matthew St. Jean.
Cover photograph by Brian Jackson / Adobe Stock.
Published by Stillwater River Publications,
West Warwick, RI, USA.

Publisher's Cataloging-in-Publication
(Provided by Cassidy Cataloguing Services, Inc.)
Names: Beard, Tim, 1968- author.
Title: Look twice : your guide to staying safe in an unsafe
world. Volume I / Tim Beard.
Description: First Stillwater River Publications edition. |
West Warwick, RI, USA : Stillwater River Publications, [2026]
Identifiers: LCCN: 2025907442 | ISBN: 9781965733615 (paperback)
Subjects: LCSH: Safety. | Accidents—Prevention. | Home
accidents—Prevention. | Dwellings—Security measures. |
Work—Safety measures. | Shopping—Safety measures. |
Transportation—Safety measures.
Classification: LCC: HV675.5 .B43 2026 | DDC: 613.6—dc23

*The views and opinions expressed in this book are solely
those of the author and do not necessarily reflect the
views and opinions of the publisher.*

DISCLAIMER

The material in this book is meant for general knowledge and informational purposes only. No legal advice or judgments are provided. If you are making important decisions or need guidance, it is always best to consult a qualified professional who can provide advice tailored to your individual circumstances.

By using the information in this book, you assume all risks and agree to indemnify and hold harmless the author and publisher from any liability, claims, damages, or issues that may arise. Always follow the laws in your country or specific jurisdiction to include federal, state and local laws. If you have any doubts, seek legal counsel to ensure you are in compliance.

The author and publisher disclaim any liability if the information contained in this book proves to be inaccurate or incomplete in any way. The content is provided "as is, " without any warranties. Always do your own research and verify details when needed.

All names, characters, and events portrayed in this book are fictitious. Any resemblance to real people, living or dead, or actual events is purely coincidental.

CONTENTS

Introduction   *ix*

PART 1: THE LOOK TWICE MINDSET
Be a Hard Target   1
It Depends....   2
Red Light, Green Light   2
Possible or Probable? You Decide....   7
Live Under the Radar   8
Listen to Your Gut   9
Know Your Patterns   10
Avoid, Avoid, Avoid   14
Limit Your Exposure   15
Find, Fix, Finish   15
The Hard Point   16
Get Off the X   19
Update Your GPS   21
Be an Instant Responder   22
When Dealing with a Threat Situation....   22
Prepare for Your Physical Response to Danger   26

PART 2: YOUR PERSONAL SECURITY
A Few Basic Thoughts   31
Clothing Choices   32
Displays of Wealth   39
Lifestyle Choices   45
Behavior in Public   46

PART 3: SAFE AT HOME
Home Selection   48
Basic Home Security Assessment   63
Improving the Security of Your Home   67

PART 4: SAFE AT WORK

Assessing Your Workplace 77

Workplace Violence 87

Preparing in Advance 91

Targeted at Work 94

PART 5: OUT IN TOWN

Overview 97

Personal Space 98

Awareness and Profiling 101

Running Errands 106

Medical Facilities and Pharmacies 116

School 118

Hanging Out with Friends 118

At the Bank or ATM 119

Community Centers 122

Parks and Exercise Paths 123

Religious Facilities 129

Large Events (Sporting Events, Concerts, Parades) 131

Night on the Town 136

PART 6: TRANSPORTATION

Automobiles 144

Subway 183

Motorcycles and Scooters 187

Electric Scooters 191

Bicycles 193

Walking and Running 195

Watercraft 200

Road Rage 203

Glossary *213*

LOOK TWICE

INTRODUCTION

INTENDED AUDIENCE

The LOOK TWICE book series is intended for regular, everyday people who are focused on living their best lives and taking care of their loved ones in this increasingly challenging world. Simply put, LOOK TWICE was written for YOU! No prior experience in security-related fields is required to understand the fundamental concepts and techniques presented in this text. This series focuses on adapting proven security concepts to everyday real-life situations and strives to present the information in a manner that is simple to understand and apply without any tactical jargon. LOOK TWICE is designed for mothers and fathers, brothers and sisters, grandparents, and aunts and uncles. It is for young adults who are moving to a big city for a new job or traveling far from home to study at a prestigious university. It is also for those who are concerned about their personal well-being, wherever they live or travel. This series is intended for the people who matter most in your life, for those you love, and for anyone who could benefit from this knowledge.

Although the concepts apply everywhere, much of this series is focused on people who live in highly urbanized cities or nearby suburbs. There has been a continuing population shift toward major city centers in pursuit of well-paying jobs, to seek renowned educational experiences and training, or to enjoy cultural opportunities that may not exist elsewhere. Cities and nearby suburbs present unique security challenges that require prior planning to effectively mitigate risk.

LOOK TWICE is not specifically intended for those with a law enforcement, military, or security-related background. Professionals from these fields may benefit from a review of the fundamentals provided in this text and their application to everyday civilian life but may also wish to seek other more advanced sources that provide higher-level technical information commensurate with their advanced skill levels and acumen in this field.

WHY SHOULD YOU READ LOOK TWICE?

Turn on the television, read your preferred online news sites, or listen to the radio. Talk with your neighbors, friends, and coworkers. It seems that all too frequently, there are heartbreaking stories about hard-working people and their loved ones who are victims of crime or violence or who get caught up in unrest sweeping through areas where they live or work. By planning ahead and applying the security concepts detailed in this text, the chances of becoming a victim can be significantly reduced. LOOK TWICE was designed to serve as a readily accessible reference guide offering clear explanations of fundamental security concepts, all drawn from the author's extensive experience over the past three decades.

HOW DO YOU USE THIS GUIDE?

You can read each volume straight through from cover to cover or focus only on the specific parts that pertain to your unique personal circumstances. **It is highly recommended to read Volume I, Part 1,** *The Look Twice Mindset,* **in its entirety** to grasp the key fundamentals that are applied throughout the entire book series. You can then pick and choose which of the remaining parts apply directly to your own situation. Use the information in your daily life; discard anything that does not work well for you or does not pertain to your daily experience. Some of the information may be relevant to you or your loved ones in the future as your personal circumstances change or your immediate environment evolves.

Scattered throughout each volume are useful **tips** and **checklists** that will help you remember essential topics and apply the information to everyday experiences. Detailed **practical scenarios and examples** deepen your understanding of the key concepts and demonstrate how they apply to real-world situations. **Insightful advice** brings the concepts to life and then shows you how to apply the lessons to your own daily routine.

PART 1

THE LOOK TWICE MINDSET

Security is essential to most aspects of life. Without security, everything is hard. At the most basic level of human needs, it is difficult to get food and water, build and protect your shelter, and keep your loved ones safe unless you have some degree of security. It is challenging to work productively and even harder to live in a peaceful, comfortable manner.

Many of us are used to taking security for granted, but this has become more and more difficult in this increasingly challenging world. The good news is that even under formidable circumstances, you can still provide a high degree of security for yourself and your loved ones through proper planning in advance of any threats.

BE A HARD TARGET

The key is to put in the time and thoughtfully examine your specific life circumstances to make yourself a **HARD TARGET**. Criminals are often looking for what they perceive as weakness, opportunity, or some clear advantage that they can exploit to produce their desired result. Your job is to look at your personal situation and change how you are perceived, lessen or eliminate vulnerabilities, and deny opportunities or advantages that a criminal might exploit. If you are a hard target, many criminals will shift their attention and choose an easier target to pursue.

This means you need to analyze your personal circumstances. You must make decisions that you are willing to live with—good or bad. Although it is possible to exist in a self-imposed, impenetrable prison-like home and never go anywhere to avoid exposure, this is most likely a bad choice and is certainly no way to live a full and productive life. Your goal is to find a balance between security and the rest of your life. Ask yourself, what level of risk am I willing to accept? By taking some basic steps, you can greatly increase your security without feeling like a prisoner or denying yourself personal freedom.

IT DEPENDS....

Fair warning: There is often not a single correct answer to solve a security problem. You may ask how you will know which option to select. A phrase you will hear again and again is "**IT DEPENDS.**" Remember, there is no one perfect solution. It depends on the specific circumstances, all the variables involved, what works best for you and your loved ones, and your personal situation. To that end, you'll learn to face the hard facts of threat situations and select a timely course of action to effectively deal with those situations.

Let's get started.

RED LIGHT, GREEN LIGHT

Everyday security is about **mitigating risk.** Everything you do in life has some degree of risk, whether it is high, medium, or low. Some risks may be unacceptably high and could lead to severe injury, death, or extremely undesirable effects. Other risks may be low and do not pose any major concerns.

As you go through this book, you will look at different aspects of life and consider potential risks and threats. You can apply a standard traffic light as a valuable tool for evaluating the level of risk for any activity:

RED: Unacceptably high risk with potentially severe impact; take action to lessen the risk

YELLOW: Medium risk; may be tolerated but is of concern and warrants continuing focus

GREEN: Acceptable risk; no major impact

This **TRAFFIC LIGHT SYSTEM** is a great tool for quick, on-the-spot evaluations of risk and for planning purposes, but remember, the level of risk can change quickly depending on the circumstances. A risk that is identified as YELLOW may quickly change to RED as the circumstances evolve. You must react and adjust your actions accordingly. Make it a habit to continuously pay attention to risk.

Gamble vs. Risk

What is a gamble versus a risk? There are many available definitions, but for our purposes, a **GAMBLE** is when you place a heavy bet by taking extreme risks that could end badly with unacceptably severe costs or even death. On the other hand, a **RISK** is a calculated decision that may result in a desired outcome, but even if the decision proves to be a failure, the consequences can still be tolerated, absorbed, or dealt with, and you "live to fight another day."

Professionals from the intelligence community take calculated risks every day to achieve mission goals; some of these risks may be quite substantial in scope and impact. True professionals, however, do not take gambles. They analyze each of the risks involved in an activity and take steps to mitigate the risks to an acceptable level. You can mirror this process in your own life to take care of your loved ones.

Although possible, it is less common for a single choice to result in a massive problem. When mitigating risk, keep in mind that **a lot of small decisions that do not have much risk by themselves can sometimes add up to an unacceptably high level of risk when combined**. This can result in a catastrophic failure. After a bad situation occurs, look back and examine what actually happened. You will often find that several poor decisions were made one after another, and when added together, they produced the final disastrous result. By evaluating each decision and mitigating the accompanying risks, we can often avoid the really big problems.

WHAT TO DO, WHAT NOT TO DO

The Concert

Dan and Seth, long-time friends and high school classmates from out in the suburbs, decided to attend a concert at the big sports arena downtown in the city. They had been waiting for months for their favorite artist to announce the concert dates and were hoping the star would make a stop in this city. The day had finally arrived, and both young men were ready to head downtown. Unfortunately, neither had good **AREA KNOWLEDGE** of the city nor any specifics about the concert venue. In their excitement and haste to see the artist perform and enjoy a fun night out on the town, both friends agreed they would just "figure it out" like they always do. All smiles and thinking only about the concert, they headed off on their adventure.

Dan borrowed his older brother's old car (no GPS), and the two quickly drove onto the main highway. As they entered the city and got closer to the sports arena, Dan noticed the vehicle was almost completely out of gasoline. He mentioned the problem to Seth, and both young men started to get irritated. Dan told Seth that he had forgotten to look the car over while still at home. He assumed his older brother had more gas in the car, so he never even looked to check the level. Now, the tank was almost completely empty. Not good. Dan said, "Let's look for a gas station before we run out of fuel." He pulled the car off at the very next exit and headed off onto the side streets. Without further warning, the car's engine sputtered to a stop, and the friends rapidly pulled over to the side of the road in a dark, unknown neighborhood. Dan and Seth had no idea where they were except that it was somewhere between home and the concert venue.

Seth reached for his mobile phone. Feeling around in his pockets and looking at the floor and the car seat, he realized he left his phone back at home on the kitchen counter. Seth said, "Dan, I forgot my phone. I almost always have it on me." Dan said, "No problem, we can just use my phone." Dan pulled his mobile phone out of his pocket to save the day, but the screen was dark, and it appeared to be turned off. Dan said, "Oh no! I forgot to charge it, and I meant to plug it in all day. I just forgot." After trying to turn the phone on, Dan realized the battery was fully depleted, and his phone was worthless at this point.

Dan and Seth chatted for a couple moments about what to do and finally decided to split up. Dan would stay with the car since he was the driver, and Seth would go on foot to look for a nearby gas station. Both young men knew this was not a welcoming area for them. Seth walked off into the darkness along a sidewalk to begin his search for fuel. Just three blocks later, on a dark side street, alone, not sure where he was going and looking confused and out of place, Seth was approached by two unfriendly men. He was violently mugged and left on the side of the road. The troubles of the night continued to mount with no end in sight.

This is an extreme case to make the point that most of these risks could have been mitigated to an acceptable level through smart preparation and a little bit of planning. If Dan and Seth knew exactly where they were going and had planned a clear route on well-traveled primary roads, filled the car up with gas in advance, brought their fully charged mobile phones, and not split up after they ran out of gas, most of these issues could have been avoided.

The key lesson here: Focus on the fundamentals, do the little stuff, pay attention to the details, mitigate risk for each step, and you are on your way to achieving success.

POSSIBLE OR PROBABLE? YOU DECIDE....

It is not viable to protect against every possible negative situation that could occur in your life. Accidents sometimes happen. Completely unforeseen situations may arise. Time and resources are limited. Unfortunately, if someone is willing to sacrifice their own life to take the life of you or your loved ones, it can be extremely difficult to stop them. So, what do you do when evaluating threats?

Consider what is **POSSIBLE** in a particular situation and then evaluate what is **PROBABLE**. Then, focus your efforts on defending against the PROBABLE. You cannot react to everything (the POSSIBLE); otherwise, you will always be reacting. In a specific situation, there may be twenty possible things that can happen. Ask yourself, what are the most probable threats in this specific circumstance? Focus your attention on these threats.

STAY SAFE

Stay Safe at the Supermarket

It is **POSSIBLE** that while driving to the store to buy groceries, your car could be crushed by a massive meteor falling from space. Is that **PROBABLE**? No. However, you remember hearing on the news that the local supermarket parking lot has had a recent rash of car break-ins.

Now you have a few choices to make since a car break-in is a much more **PROBABLE** event. One way to mitigate the risk is by choosing to park in a high-visibility portion of the parking lot with nearby direct **closed circuit television (CCTV) security camera** coverage, excellent overhead lighting, and close proximity to the front entrance of the store. You can be sure to lock your vehicle before heading into the store. You could also choose to avoid this particular shopping center completely and purchase your groceries in a different part of town on your way home from work. A third option would be to have the groceries delivered directly to your home by a delivery service.

The point is to focus on the most **PROBABLE** threats or concerns you face and then make wise choices on how to mitigate the associated risk to an acceptable level. Consider your options and then choose the best ones to lessen risk while maintaining your freedom.

LIVE UNDER THE RADAR

Everyday security may be greatly improved by living **UNDER THE RADAR**. This describes a manner of living where you deliberately seek to draw as little attention as possible and just fade into the background. You may choose to behave this way in specific situations, which will be addressed later in this book, or you may wish to adopt this strategy as an overall lifestyle if it fits with your personality and personal circumstances or needs.

An extreme version of this is known as becoming the proverbial "**GRAY MAN**." The Gray Man is an individual who goes through life without drawing much attention; this type of person is simply not memorable to the outside world. You have likely met someone at some point during your life who no one knows much about, who keeps to themselves, and who passes through your life without drawing much of a response from anyone around them. If you were to describe the Gray Man, their appearance would be "normal" or "standard" in keeping with routine cultural norms for the area where they are located and with nothing really standing out. Their hairstyle and grooming standards are average and in keeping with mild, conservative styles—nothing overly trendy. Their clothing is appropriate for the situation and is not flashy, memorable, or controversial. They are neither overdressed nor underdressed. The Gray Man fits well into his surroundings and does not pique anyone's imagination, focus, or memory. This person is just one of the hundreds of faces you might see on a regular workday or at school, and they are quite forgettable. The Gray Man is an expert at gliding through the day and all of the situations encountered and at being seen but not really "visible" to others. This person draws no lingering attention. Although the Gray Man may be very capable and fully prepared for whatever is encountered, this person is not perceived as a threat; his behavior is consistent with average expectations for the situation, and he blends in. Nothing specific separates the Gray Man from the crowd.

Living under the radar or as the Gray Man can be a challenge and is not always the best choice for everyone or for all situations. There are some circumstances, however, where it may be useful or even necessary for you to embrace this concept in order to protect yourself and your loved ones.

LISTEN TO YOUR GUT

It has been said that good judgment is the product of experience—and experience is the product of bad judgment. So, how do you develop your judgment? One way is to trust your gut instincts.

Have you ever felt the hair stand up on the back of your neck in a threatening situation? Have you ever had a "gut feeling" about a situation or a stranger, perhaps that something terrible was about to happen or that something was "off" with the person? That is likely your subconscious talking to you—pay attention!

As you build experience in life, you start to establish an idea of what is normal, what is unusual, and what may be of concern. Your subconscious is quick to identify small details that have yet to filter into your conscious awareness. By listening to your gut, you may become consciously aware of a developing situation and can adjust your responses quickly.

KNOW YOUR PATTERNS

All humans fall into patterns, whether they realize it or not. If you look at your **PATTERN OF LIFE**, you'll realize that you may awaken at roughly the same time each day and go to sleep at roughly the same time each night, perhaps altering the times a bit on weekends or if there is a special event or circumstance.

Your sleep pattern is typical of the particular patterns every human body follows for such activities as mealtimes, study habits, work hours, use of the restroom, and times for breaks. Most of us tend to have a standard pattern of places where we eat, shop, friends we visit, etc.

Why is it important to become aware of your personal patterns and routines, as well as the patterns you see all around you in your daily life? One reason is to establish a strong **BASELINE**. We can define a baseline as routine, standard patterns of behavior or events that we regularly associate with a person or situation. When something deviates from these norms or looks "out of place" for a specific environment, it may be time to investigate.

Note: Even if you pay close attention to the patterns that guide your life, it can still be difficult to break all the patterns or to become unpredictable. It requires a lot of effort and can be draining.

LOOK TWICE TIP

Baseline "Tells"

Partners generally develop an extremely strong **BASELINE** of behavior through shared experiences across all facets of life and by living in close proximity for years. This well-developed baseline makes it very difficult, if not impossible, to mislead or lie to your partner without exhibiting "tells," aka "alerting behavior."

Your partner may not know exactly what happened, but they know something is wrong or does not make sense, and the situation warrants further investigation. You may consider yourself to be a capable liar, but it is unlikely you can effectively lie to your partner or someone who is very close to you and who has developed a strong baseline about your behavior.

By developing a baseline for different people and events in your life, you can be more in tune with your environment. If something looks "off" or does not feel right, follow your intuition and observe what is happening. Quietly pay more attention, noting how the situation develops.

This effort may help you avoid becoming a victim, or it could keep you out of a problematic situation. Know what is "normal" for the area you are in. What might potential adversaries look like in areas where you live, work, or regularly find yourself? How would they likely dress or act? All of these details, along with familiarity and experience, can help you build a strong baseline from which to judge people or situations.

STAY SAFE

Is Someone Following Me?

After arriving home from running errands and while pulling into your driveway, you notice in your vehicle's rearview mirror that a car just pulled alongside the curb a couple of homes down the street from your home. No one exited the vehicle.

Having lived in your home for quite a while, you have developed a good **BASELINE** for what is normal and routine in your neighborhood; this is unusual. You are not sure why, but your intuition pokes you, and you calmly note the presence of the car without noticeably glancing toward the suspect vehicle. "That is odd," you say to yourself, knowing that all of your neighbors routinely park their cars in their driveways or garages but almost never in the street. Even visitors will usually pull into the long driveways that connect each home to the street and do not park curbside. You do not recognize the vehicle or the sole occupant.

After entering your home, you decide to investigate further. Surprisingly, the man who was driving the vehicle is still sitting inside, and it does not appear he ever exited the car. You mentally sort through the details and think to yourself that he could be on his mobile phone or fidgeting with something inside his car. Not wanting to appear paranoid, you plan to continue monitoring the situation since it strikes you as unusual. Forty minutes later, your daughter calls and needs to be picked up. You glance out the window (ensuring you cannot be seen) and observe that the car is still present, and the man is still sitting in the car. "This is getting a bit strange..." you think to yourself, but you need to pick up your daughter.

After carefully backing your car out into the street and while driving away, you observe in your rearview mirror that the parked car just pulled out after you, hanging back about half a block. You recognize this distance is just close enough for the other driver to keep you in view as you navigate the curves of the neighborhood while keeping as far back as possible. A voice in your head says, "This is not good; it looks like I may have a problem." Because **you are not paranoid if someone is actually following you**.

This example demonstrates the importance of identifying and examining personal patterns and routines since they can work both for you and against you. Others may become aware of the patterns you follow in your daily life and use that knowledge against you; this is known as **TARGETING**. If you are aware of your own patterns, you can better protect yourself and make it much more difficult for an adversary or criminal to effectively target you or your loved ones.

WHAT TO DO, WHAT NOT TO DO

An "Accidental" Encounter

Stan briefly encountered a person of interest (the target) in a grocery store, but due to circumstances beyond his control, he could only engage the target in conversation for a few brief moments before quickly departing. Stan alerted his boss about the brief meeting and was told to locate the target again. Knowing that most humans tend to fall into patterns without noticing, he constructed a plan and went back to the same grocery store again the following week. Stan chose to go to the store on the same day of the week at approximately the same time, thirty minutes before closing. This is an example of **TARGETING** based on **PATTERN OF LIFE**.

Stan was pleased to see that the target was in the store immersed in his weekly grocery shopping and was not paying attention to anything else going on around him. He later learned that the target generally shopped in the store every week on the same day and tended to procrastinate until the last possible moment, arriving roughly thirty minutes before closing. This allowed the target just enough time to gather his groceries for the upcoming week before the store closed.

The target had no idea of the pattern he was creating and how Stan could exploit the pattern to reestablish contact for his nefarious purposes. The target just thought it was an accident that he and Stan met again in the store, but this time Stan was prepared to take the conversation in a much different—and dangerous direction.

AVOID, AVOID, AVOID

One of the most important pieces of security advice is also one of the simplest in theory. To improve your security, you want to **AVOID** potential problems. This should be a major focus of your overall security posture; be proactive instead of reactive.

Look for potential problems in advance and mitigate the risk by making alternate choices and avoiding the issue altogether. Plan now to avoid problems later. As noted earlier in this chapter, no one can defend against all threats, but excellent preparation can help you avoid many. To assist in remembering and applying this essential concept, you will see the phrase **"AVOID, AVOID, AVOID"** at key points when applicable in this text.

LIMIT YOUR EXPOSURE

One way to avoid security issues is by **LIMITING YOUR EXPOSURE**. What does this mean? You want to lessen or eliminate the opportunity for an adversary to gain physical or virtual access to you or your information. To do this, you must become a hard target who is less noticeable, hard to pin down, and who offers limited attack vectors. This book will provide a wealth of techniques that will assist you in achieving these goals.

FIND, FIX, FINISH

The military has long employed a doctrine called **FIND, FIX, and FINISH** to pursue counterterrorism targets on the battlefield. Essentially, the military locates the enemy (FIND), confirms the location and pattern of life (FIX), and then takes action against the target (FINISH). Understanding this concept can help to protect you and your loved ones since criminals on the streets tend to naturally gravitate to a similar thought process (without necessarily realizing it) to pursue their targets.

Criminals are trying to **find** their targets (potential victims), figure out how and where they can get to the targets **(fix)**, and then commit their crimes at the place of their choosing (finish). If you limit your exposure, criminals will have a much harder time working through this process. If you do your job well, it is possible the criminals may just move on to an easier target.

THE HARD POINT

To protect yourself and your loved ones, you want to stay out of the reach of criminals by remaining in a **HARD POINT** when possible. Whenever you are outside of a hard point, you have increased your exposure to becoming a target or a victim of a crime to some degree. A hard point is **a location where you are generally safe or have some degree of protection—essentially a safe haven.**

Depending on certain factors that will be discussed later in this book, hard points may include your home, place of work, place of worship, or perhaps a sizable business with a lot of people on-site. It may be a facility where you are not isolated or alone, such as a hospital or a government building. A hard point is a location where you are physically separated from threats and likely out of the direct observation of aggressors. It is a place where criminals will be either incapable of pursuing you or where they will consider the environment to be too great of a risk to their goals or activities.

Once you are at a hard point, you can call for help, or there may be others present, including security professionals, who can provide prompt assistance. Although few people can stay at a hard point all the time (and who would want to?), by thoughtfully considering your exposure, you are able to better control or lessen when you may be vulnerable.

Stay Safe in a Tough Neighborhood

Mike is moving to a tough neighborhood with a well-documented history of robberies, muggings, carjackings, and violent physical assaults in the community. He would strongly prefer to live in a safer place, but his current employment for the next one to two years requires extremely long sixteen-hour days and demands his on-call availability twenty-four hours per day in case of emergency. Mike is committed to this career-enhancing job opportunity and has decided it is essential to live a few blocks from his place of work.

Mike understands this is not a great security situation, but he knows he can dramatically **mitigate the risk** involved if he examines the facts and plans ahead. First, he chooses to rent a nearby apartment with a strong on-site security presence and a secure parking garage. The garage is locked and monitored by security cameras and patrolling security guards. The doors of the apartment building require a key code to enter, and an alert doorman is posted twenty-four hours per day inside the lobby. Mike considers his apartment building to be a **HARD POINT** and feels safe at home.

Mike is very confident that his place of work is a **HARD POINT** as well. His employer has a tall, no-climb fence around the facility, along with layers of security measures inside the fenced-in area. While at work, Mike is able to focus on his job without worrying about his safety.

Although his home and place of work are both relatively secure locations, Mike knows that he still has a life to live, and he has no plans to hide inside all the time. He has to run errands and go to the grocery store, and he wants to go out now and then to meet friends or enjoy social activities as much as his time-consuming job will allow. Mike continues his planning by identifying other potential **HARD POINTS** in his local area. These are places he can go to find relative safety in case a threat situation arises while he is out in town. Mike finds a large local grocery store, a nearby hospital, and the police precinct—all places that can serve as **HARD POINTS** in case something goes wrong on the street. Mike knows that he could move rapidly to one of these facilities and seek help. All of the places have a lot of people around, and in this neighborhood, all have a security presence.

Mike makes some other decisions to help mitigate risk. He plans to run errands, when possible, during the day since crime is more likely to happen at night. When he chooses to go out to socialize, he plans to generally arrive back at home by a reasonable hour, knowing that the crime in his neighborhood tends to rise dramatically later at night, especially after midnight. When he returns to his apartment building at night, Mike remains vigilant and moves directly to his apartment (a **HARD POINT**). Mike avoids walking outside in the neighborhood to **lessen his exposure** since street crime tends to be high; instead, he prefers to move between **HARD POINTS** in his car, which is a safer option. This makes Mike a **HARDER TARGET** and keeps him out of easy reach of criminals who may wish to cause him harm.

Mike has done a good job applying the concept of **AVOID, AVOID, AVOID**. He will continue to monitor changing circumstances, stay aware of any patterns he is creating, and alter those patterns as necessary. Mike is now able to focus on his job, knowing that he has planned well and has mitigated a substantial portion of the risk he faces while living and working in his community. He will remain vigilant and adjust his plans as appropriate.

This scenario shows you how Mike applied the concepts to his own personal life situation. You can take these same concepts and now apply them directly to your life.

GET OFF THE X

Sometimes, your best efforts to thoroughly plan ahead and avoid all possible security issues are not enough, and something bad happens. What do you do when an attack happens? **GET OFF THE X**.

This may sound cryptic, but it is actually a straightforward concept. The" X" is the location where a bad situation happens: an assault, a robbery, an attempted kidnapping, or some other type of crime. To use military terms that you may have seen in war movies, the "X" is the kill zone in an ambush. When something bad is happening, your immediate goal should be to **GET OFF THE X** and move away as quickly as possible.

Criminals, terrorists, and other bad people (adversaries) often plan their activities in advance and choose a location that benefits them. The place where they choose to commit their heinous acts lends them some type of advantage. They might know the neighborhood well, live nearby, it is their "turf," there are no functioning security cameras, the police presence may be limited, the area may be especially dark at night, or it may be easy to escape after they have completed their crimes. The "X" is a place where the criminals hold all the cards, and you are at a grave disadvantage.

When you or your loved ones find yourself on the "X" and under attack, your focus should be to **GET OFF THE X** and get out of the area that the criminals have selected. You want to bust the "crime bubble" they have set up around you and move as far away as you can from the criminals and the crime scene.

How far? Remember: **IT DEPENDS**. It depends on many factors, such as the nature of the crime, where you are located, how many aggressors are present, what has happened to you, if you are injured or incapacitated, etc.

The important point is that if you are able to get outside the area that the criminals have set up for their advantage, the actual attack may come to an abrupt end, and the criminals often will not follow you. They want to commit their evil deeds at the point of their choosing, not a block down the street and around the corner where you might gain an advantage or where they might get caught or hurt. They generally do not want to follow you as you escape because they quickly lose control and run the risk of getting hurt, caught, or worse.

Remember, when attacked, whether on foot or in a vehicle, **GET OFF THE X** as quickly as possible and move to a different area to seek safety.

STAY SAFE

Stay Safe When You Get Lost

Sandy and her two young children were in the city for the day, shopping at the massive Hill Street Shopping Mall. On the way home in her SUV, Sandy missed her turn onto the interstate highway and was forced to continue down a side alley road. Running into a construction detour, Sandy quickly found herself in a local neighborhood with which she was completely unfamiliar. As darkness began to settle over the city, Sandy was growing concerned that she was lost. She knew she needed to go back in the general direction of the shopping mall to find her way onto the interstate highway.

After taking a couple more turns, Sandy pulled up to a stop sign in the local neighborhood. Without warning, several young men standing around on the street corner rushed her SUV and tried to gain entry with the door handles on both the driver and passenger sides simultaneously. Others began pounding on the side windows, and Sandy's children started crying and screaming. Fortunately, Sandy always drove with her vehicle doors locked, which kept the young men at bay for a precious few moments, but she knew they would quickly break her windows and gain entry.

Although shocked at the sudden violent attack on her vehicle, Sandy knew she had to immediately **GET OFF THE X**. She pressed the accelerator pedal to the floorboard and aimed her SUV straight down the street ahead. The heavy vehicle lurched forward, and she quickly gained speed, leaving the group of young men far behind.

After driving about a hundred yards (a football field in length) through the neighborhood, Sandy slowed down so that she did not cause a separate accident by hitting someone or something in the street. Sandy turned east and smoothly drove away from the scene of the attack. No one followed her since the young men were set up on their usual street corner, and Sandy was now well out of their grasp. Once in a safer area, Sandy regained her composure and used her GPS to guide her back to the shopping mall and eventually to her home via an alternate route.

UPDATE YOUR GPS

A GPS receiver can be a great tool for navigating in and around a city, but it is essential to make sure all available map updates are downloaded on a regular basis. Even with the updates, road construction can quickly knock you off of your route and may not be reflected on the GPS maps.

BE AN INSTANT RESPONDER

When involved in a threat situation or an attack, you are an **INSTANT RESPONDER.** First Responders are well-trained and do a great job, but they will not be standing next to you at the moment of impact on the "X." They will arrive later, possibly to clean up after the whole situation is over and done.

This means **YOU** have choices to make—**RIGHT NOW, IN THIS MOMENT.** If there is an attack or crime, it will instantly affect you or your loved ones. There is no waiting. You must rely completely on your planning, training, and on-the-spot judgment to take action that will have vast consequences going forward. **GET OFF THE X** and deal with the threat. Right now.

WHEN DEALING WITH A THREAT SITUATION....

Below are some basic factors that are common during threat situations that you should be aware of.

1) Under stress, you will revert to your prior training and experiences.

Your mind will automatically search for what to do when faced with a real-world threat situation, and you will tend to do exactly what you did in training. This is why it is so important to receive quality training, if available, and to game plan ahead of time about what could happen in a situation and how you want to respond. Planning and preparation are key to your future success. Building experience with high-quality training will help a great deal. Remember: To do a little under extreme stress, you have to know a lot. Planning and practice are keys to success. As legendary football coach Vince Lombardi said many years ago, "Practice does not make perfect. Only perfect practice makes perfect."

2) Avoid "shock" or "freezing."

When faced with an attack or a similar situation, if you do not have prior training or other information already stored in your mind, you may go into shock or freeze because you become overwhelmed by the situation. Consider for a moment that your brain is similar to a computer hard drive. Each time you undergo training or build experience, this information is written to a file in your mind's computer hard drive, providing clues about what to look for, how to react, where to go, and many other factors. The more quality training and planning you have been exposed to, the better the file will be in your mind's computer hard drive. When a threat situation happens, your mind will search this hard drive and instantly respond based on the information you have stored. If the hard drive is blank, you might freeze or take foolish, irrational actions.

3) Once an attack happens, much of your planning will fall apart due to changing circumstances.

That is OK; planning remains essential and one of your most powerful tools. Planning provides you with a framework within which to operate. It gives you a place to start, a place to adjust from. In the Marine Corps, this is referred to as Murphy's law: "Anything that can go wrong will go wrong." To counter Murphy's law, Marines use "playbooks" of standard responses for each type of mission. These playbook responses are practiced over and over until every Marine in the unit knows exactly what to do. When an actual situation happens, and the plan does not fit perfectly, Marines rely on experience and training to immediately adjust to the new circumstances, with the common planning (the playbook) serving as a starting point—a place from which to step off. This is an effective strategy to deal with the differences between planning and what actually happens during a real-world situation. You can also use this technique while planning for how you want to react if an incident happens. **"Plan ahead, and then work your plan."**

LOOK TWICE TIP

The "Eighty Percent Solution"

When facing a threat, it is better to make a good decision based on eighty percent of the information available and then take action NOW. Do not wait for a more complete picture to develop just so you can act at the perfect time LATER. Following this logic, you can continue to rapidly adjust your decisions as the situation develops to correct for changes, often outpacing your adversary's decision-making process.

Remember, PERFECT is the enemy of GOOD. Make a decision, BE DECISIVE, and move!

4) Be aware of the "Soda Straw Effect."

When under extreme stress, your body reverts back to your inner caveman or cavewoman and goes into a "fight or flight" response to protect you from the direct threat you are facing. Your field of vision (peripheral vision) dramatically shrinks from what you normally experience each day in routine situations to that of looking through a "soda straw." Your vision is laser-focused on the threat right ahead of you in the soda straw, and the rest of the field of view disappears. This is important to know because you will not be able to see to your left and right unless you physically turn your head. Once you have dealt with the threat to your immediate front, it is important to look side-to-side to assess whatever else may be going on around you.

5) Focus on the fundamentals.

The person who focuses on the fundamentals and who is really good at applying the basics in a situation will often prove victorious. Extravagant techniques and fancy, complex plans with lots of moving parts are generally best suited for movies or fiction novels, not real life. Be realistic about your capabilities and the effects that you intend to produce in a situation. Stay focused since you are protecting your most precious commodity: you and your loved ones. Concentrate on doing the basics smoothly, quickly, and effectively in order to achieve your greatest possible success. Remember the **KISS principle**: "Keep It Simple Stupid." Although blunt, this advice is time-less and sound in its logic.

LOOK TWICE TIP

Know Your 911 Protocol

If you are in an ongoing emergency situation and it is possible to call the 911 Emergency Response Line, speak with the dispatcher and provide them with the information they request. If the situation changes and you are no longer able to speak or are under duress, leave the line open (do not hang up!) and put your phone in a pocket or out of view. This may allow the dispatcher to continue to monitor and learn about the situation, inform authorities, and document the events as they unfold.

PREPARE FOR YOUR PHYSICAL RESPONSE TO DANGER

Below is a list of physical responses that may affect how you react in a threat situation. In-depth medical definitions and research concerning perception and how the body reacts under stress are broadly available online. Key details are presented below to help you understand how these concepts may affect your everyday security.

1) Night Vision

Night vision is an important topic that a lot of people do not know much about. For our purposes, we are talking about human night vision with the naked eye, not the night vision devices worn by military or law enforcement personnel during operations. Your eyes see differently at night than during the day due to the physical structure of the eye. The eye has **cones and rods** for detecting light; these are two different types of photoreceptive cells.

—**Cones:** During the day, your eye relies on the cones to see. Cones allow color vision with fine detail. Cones tend to be in the center of the retina of the eye. When a lot of light is present, you look right at an object and see the image.

—**Rods:** At night, your eye uses the rods to see. Rods only allow black-and-white vision with limited detail. Rods are concentrated on the edges of the retina, so if you look directly at an object at night, you will not be able to see it effectively. Instead, try turning your head slightly to the side and use the periphery of your eye to detect the image. Give this a try at night or in a darkened room, and you will be able to see the difference. Another key to using your eyes effectively at night is that rods are good for picking up movement. When scanning with your eyes at night, movement will stand out and quickly draw your attention. It is important to note that humans are not able to see in total darkness. There must be some light present for the human eye to detect an image.

—**To Develop Night Vision:** To develop your night vision, when the eye starts to sense a low level of light, the body produces rhodopsin or "visual purple." Although the process starts within five minutes or so, it takes roughly twenty to forty minutes to fully develop your night vision. If you are suddenly exposed to light, the rhodopsin is basically ruined, and you have to start all over again rebuilding your night vision. This is very important to know because if you are in a threat situation where you are relying on your night vision and you are suddenly exposed to a bright light such as a white flashlight or automobile headlights, you will no longer be able to see much of anything until your night vision builds back up. This could have deadly consequences.

—**Flashlights to Protect Night Vision:** The bright light of a flashlight can destroy your night vision almost immediately. Damage to your night vision can be lessened by using a red, green, or blue-green cover or filter on your flashlight. Although there is debate about which color is best and for what specific purposes, we can learn some lessons from what the military has done for many years. The most important point is not to have your flashlight illuminated too brightly, or you will still damage your night vision. A red flashlight lens cover or filter will help to protect your night vision and make it much harder to see the light from your flashlight at a distance if you are trying to conceal your location. Red does not work well with some topographic maps that are not "red light readable" due to the coloration of certain features on the charts. It is also hard to see blood with a red lens if you are injured or are providing first aid to someone who is injured. Green or blue-green flashlights are increasing in popularity and do not have the same disadvantages as red, but they offer less protection to your night vision than red light.

2) Breathing Under Stress

When you are suddenly thrust into a threatening situation and are nervous or afraid, you might find yourself holding your breath or breathing in a rapid and shallow manner. One technique to calm yourself down is to breathe deeply, fully, and intentionally as the situation allows. Center yourself. Rest assured that even experienced, highly trained professionals regularly face the effects of the fight or flight response that is hard-wired into the human body. Through experience, they learn to cope with these physical effects so that it does not hinder their ability to respond. Controlled deep breathing is an excellent tool to calm you down.

3) Managing Adrenaline

Adrenaline can be very helpful to your survival and is part of the fight-or-flight response built into the human body. When you face a threat, adrenalin is released into your body to help you deal effectively with the issue in front of you. It can make you stronger in the short term, but it comes at a price. Your fine motor skills are significantly degraded, and it becomes hard to do things that involve dexterity or any type of high-level thinking. Once you have dealt with the threat at hand, your adrenaline levels will drop. Focusing on deep breathing and calming yourself down can help you regain your dexterity and ability to think clearly. We refer to this as **PRESENCE OF MIND**—being able to think clearly under stress. Be aware of the negative effects of long-term stress and having too much adrenaline in your system over time. It can cause a different result, leading you to feel weak and lessening your physical capabilities.

4) Look Twice

When you LOOK at something, make sure that you actually SEE what you are looking at and that it registers in your brain. We can all think of an example when we looked at a sign, a car, a person, or some object or event, and then looked away. A moment later, one of your friends may have asked you, "What did the sign say?" or "What was the person wearing?" You realize that you are unsure of what you just saw, or even worse, perhaps you have no idea what the sign said or what that person you just looked at was wearing. You LOOKED, but you did not really SEE the subject of your observation. This may happen under stress or just during everyday life as you go through your day. A technique to overcome this challenge is to **LOOK, GLANCE AWAY, AND THEN LOOK AGAIN**. This can help you focus your attention and actually SEE what your eyes are examining.

CHECKLIST FOR LOOK TWICE MINDSET

___ Make yourself a HARD TARGET.
___ "IT DEPENDS."
___ Mitigate risk.
___ Take calculated risks; never take gambles.
___ When evaluating risk, consider the POSSIBLE versus the PROBABLE. Focus your attention and resources on mitigating risk from PROBABLE threats. Do not worry about every POSSIBLE threat.

___ Live UNDER THE RADAR as much as you can to avoid drawing attention. Become the GRAY MAN.

___ Understand your PATTERN OF LIFE and make changes as necessary to mitigate risk and avoid being TARGETED by those who wish to harm you or your loved ones.

___ Develop a strong BASELINE for people and events in your life.

___ AVOID, AVOID, AVOID potential problems.

___ LIMIT YOUR EXPOSURE outside of HARD POINTS to mitigate risk.

___ When facing a threat situation, GET OFF THE X and move to safety.

___ You are an INSTANT RESPONDER responsible for how you deal with a threat on the spot right now.

___ Under stress, you will revert to your prior training and experiences.

___ Avoid "shock" or "freezing" through training and by game planning ahead of time.

___ Your planning will likely fall apart at first contact with your adversary, but it gives you a place to adjust from and make decisions.

___ Remember the "Eighty Percent Solution" – be DECISIVE and move!

___ Be aware of the "Soda Straw Effect." Look side-to-side as needed to maintain awareness of what is going on around you.

___ Focus on the fundamentals and apply the KISS principle.

___ Understand how to manage the effects of night vision, breathing, and adrenaline.

___ Make sure to LOOK TWICE.

PART 2

YOUR PERSONAL SECURITY

A FEW BASIC THOUGHTS

As mentioned in Part 1, focusing on the fundamentals is a proven pathway to success in many aspects of life. This is especially true when it comes to improving your everyday personal security and that of your loved ones. Taking simple steps that are easy to understand and basic in scope can help produce the results you desire.

Throughout this book, you will see several themes repeated frequently. Here is one: **How you THINK is the most important way to protect you and your loved ones.** Although some equipment can be useful to achieve your security goals, overreliance on gear is not good. If you need some equipment, ensure that you become truly expert in every facet of its use.

Among security professionals, you will sometimes hear that "fancy gear does not make the person." You will not become a ninja just because you spend a lot of money buying high-end tactical equipment. Equipment can break, often at the worst possible moment. Batteries can fail, and you may not have a replacement handy or the time to change the battery at a critical moment. Be selective and minimize equipment whenever possible. This will also lower your "footprint" or how you appear to others. Remember that it is good to live under the radar whenever possible. You want to "hide in plain sight" and rely on yourself and your loved ones as much as you can. Appear like an everyday person. **Your most important piece of equipment is your MIND**—an agile, thoughtful, aware, and engaged mind.

In addition to your **MIND,** two other important factors that affect your personal security are your **PLANNING** prior to encountering a security threat and your **TRAINING/EXPE-RIENCE,** which will affect how you handle the situation.

This book was not written to make political or moral judgments but rather to offer insights into the security implications of making certain decisions. If you or your loved ones make life choices that draw attention or involve you in certain behaviors, you may increase your chances of also drawing unwanted attention, which can include a range of accompanying threats.

You can choose to apply all of this advice to your life, just a few items, or nothing at all. You may only wish to follow these suggestions while traveling or under certain circumstances. How and when you choose to apply this information is completely up to you and your situation. Let us look at a few of these considerations in the following sections.

CLOTHING CHOICES

Clothing choices are very personal decisions and reflect who you are, how you view the world, your likes and dislikes, and how you wish to be perceived by others. What you wear can have a substantial impact on how you are treated. Clothing choices can reflect current fashion trends, demonstrate your membership within a group or club, reflect your employment, consist of a uniform, reflect your beliefs or values, or be strictly for clothing yourself in a utilitarian manner. You may be required to wear certain clothing for different activities in your life without any real choice or ability to modify what you are expected or even required to wear. The guidelines below are just suggestions to consider for everyday security to mitigate risk. The key is to **be aware of what people generally wear in the area you are living in or visiting, and then make similar choices that are neutral and help you blend into the crowd.**

1) NO Tactical Clothing

If you want to hide in plain sight and live under the radar, **tactical clothing is NOT useful** since it will draw attention to you. People may view you as some kind of threat or assume you are carrying a weapon. You may give away the quiet advantage that you currently hold as a person who has mentally and physically prepared for potential threat situations but without having the outward appearance of being ready to walk into battle. Tactical clothing is great for a day of shooting at the range but is not a good choice if you live in the city or the suburbs and want to look like just a regular person. Do not wear military uniform items (from either current or previous eras) unless you are currently in the military and are wearing your uniform on duty.

2) Hats

Hat choices should be carefully considered. Wearing a camouflage "boonie hat" because it is sunny outside would not generally be the best choice for everyday civilian wear. Instead, purchase a wide-brimmed sun hat in a neutral or low-key color designed for civilian hikers or outdoor enthusiasts from either a sporting goods outlet or an outfitter store. Avoid tactical brands that copy military styles or patterns.

Hats are often memorable and can draw attention to you if the hat stands out or is unusual for the local area. A cowboy hat is a great example. If worn in Boston, a cowboy hat would likely draw a lot of attention. Much of this attention would probably be unwanted or negative attention due to stereotypes about those who wear cowboy hats. However, in Dallas, people wearing cowboy hats are much more common and would not be unusual to see. The hat would not draw a significant amount of attention, nor would it generate a negative reaction.

In the United States, baseball caps are commonly worn throughout the country year-round. Depending on the color, a plain baseball cap can help its wearer to blend into the crowd and conceal their appearance to a degree.

3) Sunglasses

Sunglasses can be either neutral or they can attract a lot of attention depending on the style and color of the lenses. These factors may change over time based on current fashions. Sunglasses with bright chrome-mirrored lenses, for example, are not the best choice for blending in. Sunglasses worn at inappropriate times, such as indoors or at night (for "cool factor"), may draw excessive attention and make the wearer stand out. Dark sunglasses allow you to conceal your eye movements and what you are looking at. This can be an advantage when outside on a sunny day. Sunglasses are also useful for concealing your identity and altering your appearance since they hide your eyes and break up your visible facial structure. Sunglasses can help you blend in and just be "one more face in the crowd."

4) Color Choices

Depending on the situation, you may want to choose colors that help you blend into the crowd and that do not draw attention or the eyes of others toward you. This will depend a great deal on where you are located. If you are in Miami, then fire engine red, fluorescent green, and bright yellow may be very normal, especially near South Beach. If you choose to wear all-black clothing in the middle of the day on the beach, however, you may seem out of place in the environment. On the other hand, if you are in a major city in the northeastern United States in the middle of winter going out to dinner, a black overcoat with other dark clothing may be very appropriate and even chic.

It may be best to avoid choosing a bright red ski jacket if you want to hide in plain sight and pass through the day, drawing minimal attention, even if the ski jacket is appropriate for the area. Consider choosing another more muted color that does not draw the eye to the same degree as bright red. Look at the color choices that are worn by everyday people in the area where you are spending your time and then mimic these choices. Also, observe the people who you see that stand out when you look around an area. See what is drawing your attention toward them, and then ensure you do not make these same color choices. **BLEND IN**; do not stand out. Do not buy clothing with shockingly bright colors unless that is the standard for the area you are in. Do NOT wear tactical colors if avoidable (desert tan, coyote, olive drab, military or hunting camouflage patterns, etc.) These colors are less common in the city or suburbs. Hunting camouflage is widely worn in some areas but is less common in many larger cities, depending on what part of the country you find yourself in. Always use your best judgment.

5) Controversial or Political Statements or Logos

If you want to mitigate risk by blending in and avoiding attention, choose clothing without any controversial or political statements or logos. In modern America, you can be confident that if you wear clothing adorned with a political statement that you support, you will, in a short period of time, cross paths with someone who is offended by the statement or logo. **What is great for you may be offensive to others.** This includes ballcaps or T-shirts with the name and logo of your favorite brand of ammunition or firearm, logos that indicate a political affiliation or group, support for a particular political candidate or party, or a certain stance on a volatile political issue. Also, avoid advertising for a hobby, a club, or even a company that brands you as a member of a certain group or political persuasion. Even sports team logos, jerseys, or paraphernalia can prove volatile if you are supporting "the wrong team" in a different city or an area where that team is unpopular and draws out strong emotions. As a general rule of thumb, **when possible, choose clothing in solids or patterns without any controversial wording or logos.**

6) Footwear

You can tell a lot about someone by the shoes that they choose to wear. Many women are experts at accessorizing with shoes and know how important shoes are to completing an outfit. Some men may also have this knowledge and enjoy owning a wide variety of shoes, while others instead choose to have only a few pairs of shoes that they wear all the time.

For your purposes, consider the utility of the shoes for different situations in which you might find yourself. Think for a moment if your shoes are up to the task in the following situations: if you have to run to safety, kick someone to defend yourself, maintain footing under slippery circumstances such as a wet or greasy tile surface or on ice, protect your ankles on rugged ground, or wade through water, for example. Few shoes are the perfect choice for all situations, but keep in mind the strengths and limitations of each type of shoe.

If you are dressed for a formal or business occasion, your shoes may have some limitations of which you need to be aware. Some traditional shoes may be slippery depending on the sole of the shoe. Other modern dress shoes may have a sole similar to athletic shoes and will offer greater traction. If a woman is wearing high heels and needs to run to safety, she will likely have to kick off her heels first and then continue in bare feet. To enhance mobility and security, ladies may wish to wear a pair of flats or other shoes with some degree of traction when going to or from work or an event instead of wearing high heels and then switching over to heels after arriving at the event.

Cowboy boots have been worn by the stars of many action movies over the years. These boots are generally not the best choice for fighting or running and can be very slippery on wet floors such as tile or smooth concrete, depending on the sole featured on the boots. Although cowboy boots can be appropriate in certain areas of the country where they are a cultural staple, in other big cities or parts of the country, wearing cowboy boots may be a red flag that causes you to stand out as an outsider who is new to the city or just visiting. An adversary may notice the boots and view you as a softer target who likely does not know the area as well as a local.

Military boots are very identifiable and are not the best choice due to their tactical appearance. They will tend to draw attention and not help you blend in if you are trying to avoid drawing scrutiny.

Hiking boots have a lot of advantages for ankle protection and for maintaining your footing. Many styles are bulky, however, and may not fit in well for some urban environments. Some hiking boots are waterproof when lined with a specialized fabric, which can be an advantage. Keep in mind that this type of waterproof fabric works both ways: it keeps water out, but if water comes in over the top of the shoe or boot, it also keeps water in. It may take a few days to get your boots to dry out thoroughly if they fill with water for some reason.

Athletic shoes may be an excellent choice, depending on the environment, shoe style, and color, due to their functionality and great tread properties. Athletic shoes tend to be widely worn everywhere and blend into most environments. Due to current styles, you may choose to not tie your shoes or even remove the laces. This can reduce the utility of the shoe since the shoes may fall off if you have to run or you may trip over the untied laces.

7) Inappropriate Clothing

The definition of what is considered inappropriate clothing varies depending on the region of the country where you are living or visiting. A thong swimsuit, for example, is a very common sight on the beaches in South Florida. The same swimsuit worn at a lake in the Midwest might result in an arrest for indecent exposure or draw a lot of unwanted attention because it violates local laws or norms. Styles of clothing that may be appropriate in New York City or Los Angeles may not fit well in San Antonio or Atlanta. Be aware of these differences when making clothing selections to avoid drawing unwanted attention.

Choose clothing appropriate for an event. You probably would not choose to wear fitness attire to an evening cocktail party. You also would likely not choose to wear professional business attire for a workout at the gym or to go hiking in the woods.

Keep these suggestions in mind to assist you with **blending in** and **living under the radar**.

DISPLAYS OF WEALTH

Driving an expensive vehicle, wearing high-end prestige clothing or jewelry, carrying a designer handbag, or wearing an expensive watch are all **displays of wealth** that may be important to you for a multitude of reasons. It is essential to understand the potential security ramifications of these choices because, in many cities and suburban areas, there may be very real consequences.

Criminals often target people who display expensive items that could be stolen and later resold. There have also been numerous examples of criminal gangs conducting **"follow home robberies,"** targeting individuals at locations where the wealthy shop or spend their time and then following the person to a location where they can be isolated, such as their home or small business. The criminals then rob the person of all items of value, sometimes injuring the person for no apparent reason as they complete the robbery. Let us look at the following scenario to better understand this disturbing trend and apply some of the security lessons we have learned.

WHAT TO DO, WHAT NOT TO DO
Unwanted Visitors

Alex and Maria wanted to spend some time celebrating together on Saturday after a busy and successful week of work. Alex had just won a major case in court for a large corporate client and was expecting this victory would finally help him to make partner at the blue-chip law firm where he worked. Maria owned a trendy art studio downtown and had just held a successful art exhibition for a few up-and-coming local artists earlier in the week, selling several of the artists' paintings. Alex and Maria were excited at their career success and the accompanying wealth they were building together.

The couple decided to go out for a late lunch at their favorite restaurant in an upscale area of town near the marina. Pulling up to the restaurant, Alex handed the keys of his gleaming, high-end German sports car over to the valet. Alex and Maria entered the restaurant for their reservation, not noticing the man sitting on the nearby park bench who was watching their every move, as well as other patrons who might be good "targets." The man was a non-descript lookout for one of the local notorious criminal gangs that had been successfully committing crimes against everyday citizens in the city for years. He took note of the expensive sports car, as well as the designer clothing that Alex and Maria were both wearing. The lookout could not help but notice the expensive watch on Alex's wrist and the designer handbag that Maria was carrying. As soon as the couple entered the restaurant, the lookout placed a call on his mobile phone to his friends. "We got a live one," he told his friends. "Get ready."

Alex and Maria enjoyed a nice lunch, catching up on the events of the week and sharing details of their individual successes. Unbeknownst to them, the local criminal gang was busy setting a trap for their prey. The gang prepositioned four members in an SUV half a block from the restaurant. The SUV was prepared to follow Alex and Maria and look for an isolated location to rob them. The lookout told the crew that since Alex and Maria were wearing what looked to be expensive clothing and jewelry, there was a good chance they were likely carrying a lot of money or credit cards. The gang was excited, and their presence had not been detected.

After paying the bill, Alex and Maria exited the restaurant, and the valet drove the sports car up to the front door with an attention-getting roar. Instead of heading directly home, Alex and Maria decided to go to a nearby luxury shopping mall to make a few purchases. Fully engaged in conversation and further distracted by the car stereo playing in the background, neither Alex nor Maria noticed the SUV pull out from the parking spot along the side of the road and start to follow them as they drove past. Their car would be easy to follow since it was an unusual, flashy model with a unique custom license plate: "WIN4YOU", referring to Alex's work as an attorney.

The gang in the SUV were planning their next move as they drove. One member suggested running into the back of the car at a stop sign on a remote side street if the opportunity presented itself. He noted that the gang had used this technique in the past to get the passengers to stop and exit their vehicle, where they were violently assaulted and robbed on the sidewalk. It had been a quick, successful robbery.

The leader of the gang was patient and suggested following the couple for a little while to see where they went. He was hopeful to land a bigger score than just what was in the car. Suddenly, the sports car turned into the parking lot at the shopping mall. The SUV continued straight down the road so that they would not alert Alex and Maria to their presence.

Alex and Maria parked their car in the parking lot and walked into the shopping mall, unaware of the scrutiny they were under. The couple had several items they wanted to purchase. This afforded the gang plenty of time to set up on the car and rework their plan.

While the couple enjoyed the shopping trip, the SUV

carefully circled around the block and methodically combed through the parking lot, looking for the sports car with the custom license plate. It did not take them long to find the car, and they set up again adjacent to a nearby parking lot exit where they could naturally and smoothly pull out to follow the car.

Alex and Maria walked back to their vehicle, both texting on their phones while trying simultaneously to manage the shopping bags from their purchases. With their attention riveted to their mobile phones, the couple was oblivious to the intent stares from the occupants of the SUV parked only forty feet away. Alex started up their car and smoothly pulled out of the parking lot, heading to the couple's home. Moments later, the SUV followed, hanging back just enough to avoid drawing any significant scrutiny.

Alex drove smoothly through traffic. Not long after, the couple pulled into the driveway of their home just after darkness began to settle over the neighborhood. The gang leader was glad he had been patient since this was now going to be a much more lucrative robbery. He cautiously followed Alex into the driveway. The four men quickly exited the SUV and entered the home's garage before the garage door could be lowered. Alex and Maria were violently assaulted and robbed by the four men in their own home. The gang filled the SUV with the most expensive items from the home, moving briskly but with limited concern about getting caught.

As they prepared to depart, the gang leader looked over at Alex and thought about the special vanity plate "WIN4YOU" on the sports car. The gang leader said, "It looks like today was actually a WIN FOR ME." He laughed and walked out the door. The gang departed and disappeared into the darkness.

WHAT TO DO, WHAT NOT TO DO:

Although simply trying to enjoy their lives and the fruits of their professional success, Alex and Maria made several errors that led to the terrible attack in their home. By choosing to display their wealth in a flashy manner by driving an expensive, high-end sports car, wearing luxury designer clothing, and frequenting prestigious venues known for wealthy clientele, Alex and Maria consciously opted to live ABOVE the radar and STAND OUT. No one is suggesting that the couple should live on a tight budget and not enjoy some nice things. It might be smart, however, to step back and look at the overall image they are presenting to others around them. Significant displays of wealth are like a magnet for those who want to take your blessings from you. By choosing to drive a more moderate but less flashy vehicle instead of a six-figure, highly desirable imported sports car ready for a professional car race, Alex would not have attracted such a large amount of attention.

When maneuvering around town on foot and while driving, the couple would have been well served to eliminate distractions and pay closer attention to the activities going on in their vicinity. It is hard to notice if others are closely watching you when your focus is directed to your mobile phone while walking out of the shopping mall. Put the phone away, keep your head up, and watch what is going on. You are vulnerable to a smash-and-grab robbery when distracted and carrying numerous packages, many of which are likely valuable. Pay attention to what is going on around you.

When the couple was approaching their home, they needed to increase their vigilance and watch closely to see if anyone followed them from town. If you live in a relatively quiet neighborhood or have at least established a strong baseline for what is normal in your community, it is much harder for an adversary to follow you all the way to your driveway. If you are unsure if you are being followed, do not drive to your home. Instead, drive to a local police precinct or, at a minimum, to a populated location where you are not isolated.

Once you decide to approach your residence, pay close attention when entering your garage or front door and make sure no one follows. Always stay aware of your surroundings and maintain positive observation until the garage door is closed/locked or you have entered and locked your door. Some of these points are simple and easy to accomplish, but when distracted or stressed, many people forget to take these little steps and present an adversary with a possible opportunity to exploit.

LOOK TWICE TIP

Why is that person still sitting in their vehicle?

Be aware of parked vehicles where the occupant(s) sit for long periods in the vehicle or at strange hours of the day, and do not exit the vehicle in a timely fashion. This is of increased interest if the vehicle is parked in a location where it would be unusual to see occupants remain with the vehicle for a lengthy period of time.

This type of behavior could point to several things: law enforcement, criminal activity, surveillance of some type, a stalker, or it could be something harmless such as a person simply talking on their mobile device for a long time. The key point is that this type of behavior warrants further attention or observation, especially if the occupants are multiple men. If you have a good BASELINE for what is normal and what is unusual in the area, you may notice unusual behaviors more quickly.

LIFESTYLE CHOICES

Below are a few lifestyle choices worthy of your consideration. You can choose to closely adhere to this guidance, completely discard it, or walk some middle ground. The choice is yours, but so are the consequences. The decisions you make should reflect the level of security you are trying to achieve in your life and the nature of any threats that you face.

1) SIMPLIFY YOUR LIFE to improve your security.

Stay out of view and under the radar as much as possible, only appearing for brief periods when you need to be out in town. Spend the bulk of your time at **HARD POINTS,** such as your home, place of work, or with family. These are environments where you can generally control your exposure, including how much you are seen, by whom, and who is allowed to be around you and your loved ones. This is most applicable to those facing significant threats or who live in a dangerous area.

If you opt to spend a lot of your time out in town at stores, in public social locations such as cafes, parks, restaurants, shopping malls, or nightclubs, you increase the exposure time that someone is able to "get at you." You are providing a potential aggressor with additional locations and situations where they can attempt to target you or your loved ones. Depending on your security profile, this could have difficult ramifications. **The less visible you are, the harder it is to "spot" you or effectively target you.**

2) Seek to improve your level of PHYSICAL FITNESS.

If you are already fit, maintain your high standards. If you are not in optimal condition, work to improve your level of fitness as much as you can; your body and overall health will thank you. If you appear physically fit, you are generally regarded as a harder target by criminals and more likely to be left alone in favor of weaker, less prepared targets. A high level of physical fitness alone will not save you in a threat situation, but it is a factor that works to your advantage.

3) Involvement with any ILLICIT ACTIVITIES significantly affects your everyday security.

If you or your loved ones make life choices that bring you into contact with illegal drugs, gambling, stolen property, prostitution, etc., then you are exposing yourself to a range of security issues that increase the likelihood of trouble. Many of these activities involve people who are desperate to fill their needs. Keep in mind that even if you have no direct participation in or knowledge of these activities, if one of your loved ones is involved, then you may still feel the sting of their choices in your own life. **Trouble will often find you in life; you do not have to go looking for it.** These choices will make your life harder and more complicated.

BEHAVIOR IN PUBLIC

Always consider your profile when in public. How do you appear to others with whom you come in contact? **Do you walk deliberately and with confidence?** Are you or others with whom you spend your time loud and boisterous? Or do you quietly travel along the path of life each day, treating others with courtesy and politeness? All of these choices have a direct impact on the amount of attention you draw and how you are perceived by others. Gravitate toward a public profile that is understated, quiet, polite, and does not actively seek to be the center of attention. Blend in and live under the radar.

CHECKLIST FOR YOUR PERSONAL SECURITY

___ How you THINK is the most important way to protect you and your loved ones.

___ The most significant factors for your personal security are your MIND, PLANNING prior to encountering a security threat, and your TRAINING/EXPERIENCE.

___ Be aware of what people generally wear in the area that you are living in or visiting and make similar choices that are neutral and help you to blend into the crowd.

___ Be cautious about DISPLAYS OF WEALTH and the attention they may attract.

___ SIMPLIFY YOUR LIFE to improve your security.

___ The less visible you are, the harder it is to "spot" you or effectively target you.

___ Seek to improve your level of PHYSICAL FITNESS.

___ Involvement with any ILLICIT ACTIVITIES may produce significant repercussions on your everyday security.

___ Always consider your profile when in public. Choose to blend in and live under the radar.

PART 3

SAFE AT HOME

Your home is your castle. It is a place where you should feel comfortable. Your home should also be a HARD POINT where you are generally safe or have some degree of protection—essentially a safe haven. If you already have a home and do not plan to move any time soon, this chapter will offer some ideas about how to "harden" your current residence and make it more secure. If you are moving to a new city and plan to rent or purchase a different place to live, carefully consider the advantages and disadvantages of various types of homes since your selection will have an impact on your everyday security.

HOME SELECTION

When selecting a home in a new city, there are numerous factors to consider. Each style or type of home may satisfy some security requirements while exposing the owner to other security concerns. Let us examine several different types of homes and consider the associated security variables. This is not an all-inclusive list; remember, it is important to focus on PROBABLE threats that you might face and not waste time on POSSIBLE threats that are not pertinent to your personal situation.

1) Single-Family Home

Like many people across the country, you may dream of owning a detached single-family home. When renting or purchasing this style of residence, it is preferable that the home includes an enclosed garage to control access and provide some degree of protection for vehicles. Under the best of circumstances, the garage would be directly attached to the home, but a separate stand-alone garage building located in close proximity to the home will also work well. It is becoming much more difficult for many Americans to purchase a single-family home due to skyrocketing real estate prices in many cities. If you can afford it, there are several security advantages to owning or renting a single-family home.

ADVANTAGES

—**Controlled access to the interior of the home.** An important advantage is controlled access. Only you or your loved ones are allowed in the home unless you authorize access to others. No one else has a key or an access code unless you choose to give them a copy or provide a code.

—**Privacy.** This is one of the greatest advantages of a single-family home. It is easy to have private conversations and keep your activities and those of your loved ones away from the unwanted attention and prying eyes of outsiders. This is especially true if the home has a basement, which provides further protection from observation and limits sound proliferation.

—**Garage.** If your home has a garage with a secure locking garage door, you are able to protect your vehicle more capably from theft, vandalism, and sabotage. An attached garage with a remote-controlled door also allows you to drive up to your home, open the door by remote, pull in, and shut the garage door, all prior to exiting your vehicle. You can then safely enter your home from a well-lit garage without exposing yourself to any direct threats from the street or a darkened driveway. This same arrangement can enable private visits to your home by guests or friends, if you choose, and prevent the prying eyes and overactive imaginations of nosey neighbors from keeping track of who comes and goes from your home.

—**Security devices.** You can install security devices if you choose. Equipment may include a professionally monitored alarm system, indoor/outdoor security cameras with motion detectors and night vision, motion-activated exterior lighting, window or door modifications, advanced high-security door locks, or other devices to "harden" your home.

—**Egress.** If you need to exit your home due to a security threat or a fire, the numerous windows and doors offer several different routes to escape in various directions.

CONCERNS

—**Ground Floor Access.** Unlike a condominium unit in a high-rise building with limited access, a single-family home is built directly on the ground with numerous entry points, which could be exploited by an adversary. This type of structure can be attacked from the front, back, and perhaps the sides or basement, depending on the location of windows, doors, or other access points. The protection of each entry point must be addressed in any comprehensive security plan.

—**Theft and vandalism in exterior areas.** Items from the yard and back patio area are subject to theft or vandalism. This could include an expensive BBQ grill, garden hose, decorative items, or yard furniture. On a positive note, at least you can own a BBQ grill in a single-family home, whereas a charcoal or gas grill is usually against the local fire code to even own or possess if you live in a condo or apartment. There is always a trade-off!

Regarding theft, there is one downside to having a garage, especially an attached garage. If a criminal gains access to your garage while you are away from home, they can conceal their vehicle from outside view while robbing your home and loading the vehicle at their convenience. This plan can be foiled by applying other security measures to your home to ward off burglars and detect any break-ins.

—**Observation.** Depending on how visible your home is from the street, it may be relatively easy for an adversary to conduct surveillance on you or your loved ones. Such adversaries could include criminals who are casing your home prior to a robbery or other crime, a stalker, or a business competitor, depending on the nature of your work. By observing your home, criminals may be able to glean information about your schedule, PATTERN OF LIFE, or if you are away on travel out of town.

—**Packages and mailbox.** Unless you have a way to properly secure packages delivered to your porch, you may have to contend with "porch pirates." These criminals steal packages left unattended or unsecured on porches, especially if the packages are visible from the street. Some porch pirates may follow not far behind a delivery truck, and after observing a delivery, they will promptly steal packages that were even concealed from view. Criminals may also target your stand-alone mailbox in front of your home to steal packages and other mail, especially around major holidays. It is easy to steal from these mailboxes since they are unlocked, and the mail is left exposed. This type of theft is much less likely if your mail is delivered to a cluster mailbox that services multiple homes in the community since each individual mailbox has its own separate lock. If you have a more extreme security profile, an unsecured stand-alone mailbox can allow an adversary to easily hand-deliver and conceal a mail bomb or some other type of nefarious package directly to your home.

—**Trash.** If an adversary sifts through your trash after it has been placed curbside for pick-up, they can learn a lot of detailed information about you, including who is living in your home and your activities. This technique is commonly used by both law enforcement and criminals depending on the specific target and each group's information collection goals. In the case of a single-family home, it is highly PROBABLE that all of the trash is directly produced by the residents of the home or their guests; the trash is most likely not mixed in with trash from other homes like in a condo or apartment building. In a condo setting, each resident drops their trash into one of the community trash chutes, which all empty into large community dumpsters for pick-up. This arrangement makes it more difficult to determine what trash belongs to which resident or condo unit. When throwing out any trash from any type of residence, always keep this vulnerability in mind.

LOOK TWICE TIP

Safely Dispose Papers and Mail

Never throw any paper into your trash. Invest in a quality, professional crosscut business shredder for a couple hundred dollars from an office supply company and use it daily to shred any papers you no longer need. A crosscut shredder shreds paper into small pieces that cannot be easily reassembled, unlike a standard strip shredder. If your security needs are much higher, ensure the crosscut is so small that papers cannot be reassembled, even with specialized computer analysis software. The highest security shredders are very expensive and will disintegrate papers into a form that closely resembles dust.

Shred all mail that is labeled with your name and address, along with all paper bills, receipts, notes, letters, lists, prescription medicine labels—anything with writing on it that could provide insights into your life. If you need to keep any of this material, scan it into your electronic files and shred the original paper. This frees up space in your residence, is more secure, and eliminates much of the information that can be gleaned from your home's trash.

Another tip to save time: put all of the paper into a designated "shred bag" (a trash bag that you maintain only for this purpose) throughout each day and then just shred it all at once on a single day each week.

2) Townhome or Multi-Family Home

Townhomes and multi-family homes have many of the same advantages and concerns as single-family homes. There is generally a reduction in privacy when compared to single-family homes since the units are built in closer proximity, and each residence shares at least one wall with a neighbor. Depending on the quality of construction, some townhomes and multi-family homes may allow conversations to drift through shared walls. This style of home has fewer windows and doors from which to exit in case of emergency due to the shared walls on each side. All exits will be either in the front or the back of the home. An end unit will have additional windows available on one side of the structure.

3) Condominium and Apartment Buildings

Condominiums and apartments have similar advantages and concerns but with one significant distinction between the two types of buildings: condominiums have individual unit owners, while apartments are generally owned by a company, and each individual apartment is leased (rented) for a specific period of time. Condo buildings tend to have a different feel to them since the bulk of the residents own the units where they reside rather than just lease them. This results in a less transient population in the building and can translate into a different set of security issues.

ADVANTAGES

—**Controlled access and limited observation.** Many condo or apartment buildings are set off from the street with a security presence providing some form of visitor screening at an entry control point (guardhouse). This limits or prevents unidentified visitors without a defined purpose from accessing the property or even getting close to the building. Once you enter the parking garage or the condo/apartment building, an adversary loses the ability to continue to observe your movements; unless the adversary follows you inside, you essentially disappear until you choose to depart the building.

—**"Fortress in the Sky."** If you are located on the third floor or higher, it may be difficult to gain access to your unit from the outside of a condo/apartment building. Depending on the design of the building's balconies, it could be a great challenge to maneuver from one balcony to a neighboring balcony, requiring the skills of a ninja and making this feat only POSSIBLE but not PROBABLE. In some cities, condo/apartment buildings have fire escapes mounted on the outside of the structure, which removes this height advantage and instead turns it into a disadvantage and a security concern all on its own. Look and see how your building was constructed. Either way, ensure you secure your windows and any sliding doors from the inside to enhance your security. Sliding doors can be effectively secured by placing a thick wooden dowel rod or a metal bar inside the lower track in the threshold at the bottom of the door along the floor. This bar effectively prevents an adversary from forcing the door open along the track. They would have to cut or break the glass to gain entry through the door, which is a much tougher and likely noisier feat.

—**Professional staff and neighbors nearby.** If there is a medical emergency or a security incident, there are professional staff employed by the property management along with numerous neighbors in close proximity who you can call for rapid assistance.

CONCERNS

—-**Privacy.** Living in a dense community with lots of neighbors, privacy can be elusive. It is difficult to have truly private conversations since "the walls have ears." It is easy to hear a conversation near a unit's front door or through the ceiling or walls, depending on the quality of the construction of the building. If voices are raised, the conversation will easily extend through the entry door and into the hallway. It is next to impossible to host private visitors since their arrival and departure will be captured on multiple security cameras in the lobby, elevator, and possibly even the hallway near your unit, depending on the building's security plan. Your daily routine is generally on display to your neighbors. Nearby neighbors will smell the food you are cooking for each meal, and they will hear your footsteps when you awaken in the morning. They will also hear silence (a lack of footsteps) after you go to sleep at night. If you are away on travel, the absence of muffled voices or any footsteps will be a good tip-off that your unit is unattended. Other residents in the building, many of whom you may not even know, may quietly watch every public move you make as you go about your day or come and go from the building.

—**Access to the interior of the condo or apartment unit while you are away.** Depending on building policy, you may be required to allow workers and outside contractors entry into your unit even when you are not at home. This could include pest control technicians, building maintenance workers, plumbers, or others when the property management determines there is a "need." Although generally accompanied by a security guard or member of the building staff, this access may not be desirable nor work to your advantage.

—**Egress.** In a high-rise building, egress can be difficult in an emergency. There is generally only one entry door into a unit. If you are inside your unit and your entry door is blocked for some reason, you have a problem. In case of a fire emergency, egress may be further complicated if the elevators are out of service. This scenario would require you to make a long descent via the stairwell, which might prove physically difficult for some individuals, especially those with special needs.

—**Fire**. If one of your neighbors accidentally starts a fire while cooking in their unit in a condo or apartment building, your chances of being affected are much greater than would be expected in a single-family home or even a townhome. Fire can spread more easily within a condo/apartment building than between single-family homes that are separated by much greater distances. Townhomes are usually required by construction code to have a fire barrier built into the wall between units.

—**Parking Garage.** If you are fortunate enough to have a private garage facility as part of your condo or apartment building, it will only offer limited security compared to a single-family home or townhome with an enclosed, private garage. The parking garage for a condo/apartment building still allows other residents and their guests direct access to the vicinity of your vehicle. You may be surprised at the number of workers or guests from outside of your community who pass through the parking garage each day for any of a multitude of reasons. A parking garage is better than curbside parking on the street or in an open parking lot. It may have security camera coverage or security patrols, but it does not fully protect access to your vehicle.

—**Short-term rental websites.** Instead of living full-time in their condos, some owners post their units on specialized websites that offer short-term rentals in popular destinations around the world. This can present security concerns for you or other residents who live in the condominium building. One concern is that the rented unit will attract new people from outside the community for short periods of time; these people may turn over every few days or each week. The background and history of these renters are mostly unknown, and they are not personally invested in the well-being and protection of your community. Another concern is that some renters, especially in major tourist destinations such as Miami or New York City, may use the unit for illicit activities. This type of short-term rental is unlikely to occur in a single-family home or townhome community where most people reside full-time or have long-term rentals lasting in excess of a year.

4) University Dormitory

If you are a student, you may choose to live in a dorm room for several reasons. University policy may require all first-year students to live on campus in dorms, for example. The option for living in a dorm room during sophomore to senior years of school may be based on a lottery or some other selection system and varies from campus to campus. Another reason may be affordability. You might appreciate the connection to other students going through the same course of study or enjoy the overall dorm experience. Many of the security advantages and concerns mentioned in the **"Condominium and Apartment Buildings"** section apply to university dorms due to their similar building construction. Some additional security thoughts are discussed below.

ADVANTAGES

—**Proximity to campus.** Dorms are generally located on university property, which, in the case of a city campus, puts your residence in close proximity to classroom buildings, the university library, and other important facilities. If you do not live in the dorms, then you will have to live off-campus without the security protections offered by the university. Living in the dorms will shelter you from many of the security concerns that you might experience in other areas of a major city. City campuses are generally a unique enclave within the town where they are located. While living in a dorm, you will not have to travel as far and will have less exposure to some security risks. You may not even need a vehicle to move about campus due to the small footprint of many schools. Everything you need will be within walking distance, including grocery or convenience stores, medical facilities, and shops that cater to you and other members of the university population.

—**Security protections.** Most universities have an on-campus police department whose mission is to protect and serve the student population and ensure the security of all campus facilities. University grounds often have additional security lighting, cameras, and other features not broadly available throughout the rest of the city. Administrators tend to cater to the unique security needs of the student population. They are well aware that if you feel the campus is a dangerous environment, you and other current or prospective students may think twice about attending the school.

—**Outsiders are easier to spot.** Since the student population tends to be relatively homogenized by age and each university tends to have a certain personality associated with its student body, it may be easier for you to spot outsiders. Outsiders include non-students, people from other universities, or potential criminals from other parts of the city looking to prey on the student population. Be wary when encountering outsiders hanging around the campus for no apparent reason.

CONCERNS

—**Drugs and alcohol.** Like many college students, you may be away from home for the first time in your life and experiencing a new level of freedom. It is common on many university campuses for students to have significantly higher levels of exposure to drug and alcohol use, even if they are trying to avoid any contact. Although these issues are widespread and include dorms, drug and alcohol abuse may be even more prevalent when living off-campus with the additional freedom offered by an apartment or a home separated from the university grounds. Substance abuse can invite other security threats as well.

—**Inexperienced student population.** Some criminals focus on targeting college campuses because of the perceived inexperience and youthfulness of many students. Criminals may view you or other students as an "easy mark" or a "soft target" with limited experience in the city. The university student body may be viewed as a vulnerable population for exploitation.

WHAT TO DO, WHAT NOT TO DO

Time's Up

Trey was a freshman engineering student at a nationally known university in a major Southeastern US city. He had just finished eating dinner at a local burger shop down the street with a few of his classmates and was walking alone back to his nearby dormitory. Deep in thought about a project he was completing for one of his classes, Trey felt the cold, blustering winter wind slice through the darkness of the evening air. He pulled up the zipper on his heavy winter jacket and crossed the street at the crosswalk, unaware of the eyes now following his every move. Trey continued to walk toward one of the rear dormitory entrance doors. An anonymous figure clad in a dark parka and ski hat briskly moved toward Trey in the darkness.

As Trey approached the dorm's heavy, locked metal door, he dug his hand into his pocket, searching for his key. A friendly voice called out from just behind him in the dark, "Excuse me...do you know what time it is?" Without glancing at the voice, Trey raised his expensive wristwatch to check the time and said, "It is 7:45 p.m." The watch was a gift from his family to celebrate his high school graduation and his admission to the top institute.

Without warning, Trey felt the air pushed out of his lungs as the anonymous figure slammed his body into the brick wall next to the security door. The attacker was much bigger and stronger than Trey, and the sheer violence and suddenness of the attack were overwhelming. The attacker pressed Trey's face into the brick wall so that he could not move his head.

The attacker yelled, "Give me your watch!" Trey tried to reason with the attacker and said it was a special gift. The attacker bellowed, "Shut up!" and grabbed the watch off of Trey's wrist. Leaning his heavy, muscular body against Trey's back, the attacker easily pinned him to the wall. He reached into Trey's back pocket and removed his wallet. The attacker harshly grabbed Trey's throat and felt for a necklace. He ripped a gold chain and crucifix from Trey's neck. Trey begged him not to take the chain and said, "It is a family heirloom; please don't take it!" The anonymous attacker laughed, gave Trey one last shove into the wall, and ran into the darkness.

With tears of shock, anger, and fear streaming down his face, Trey fumbled about in his pocket for the key, unlocked the door, and ran into the dorm hallway. He yelled, "Help—I just got mugged!" Several other students came to his aid and immediately rushed outside to look for the anonymous attacker in the cold winter darkness, but he was long gone. The attacker was never caught.

WHAT TO DO, WHAT NOT TO DO:

Although not mentioned in the scenario, Trey was not from this city. He was from a small town out of state and did not have a lot of experience dealing with some of the unfortunate rigors of big-city life. The best way for you to deal with this type of situation is to **AVOID, AVOID, AVOID**. Trey was only walking a short distance between the burger shop (a relatively safe location) and his dorm (**HARD POINT**), but he was **exposed** between these two points and needed to remain fully aware, perhaps choosing to walk with another student or two. He should have kept his head up and eyes scanning the vicinity around him, especially since he was moving alone in the dark city at night. Trey needed to maintain mental discipline and would have been well-served to keep his focus on his immediate surroundings and save his deep thoughts about the unfinished class project for later on in the safety of his dorm room. By appearing observant, focused, and walking deliberately with purpose, Trey could have projected an air of confidence and would have come across to an observer as a **HARD TARGET**. The attacker might have selected another person to pursue instead of Trey.

When the anonymous figure asked Trey about the time, he should have looked at the person first to rapidly evaluate the situation while maintaining a protective distance. Trey could have said in a firm, clear voice, "No, I do not have the time," while moving swiftly toward safety. The attacker used a standard ploy to distract the inexperienced student while confirming that Trey had an item of value to steal (the wristwatch). Once the powerful attacker overwhelmed the much smaller student, the situation spiraled out of Trey's control, and all hope was lost. **Remember that money and possessions are not worth your life. Things can be replaced; YOU cannot** be replaced. **Do your best to observe key data about the overall attack and specifics about the attacker** to report later to law enforcement. Apply the basic security concepts detailed in this book and **avoid exposure** to this type of difficult circumstance entirely.

BASIC HOME SECURITY ASSESSMENT

Working through the basic assessment process can help you identify vulnerabilities and build an improved security plan. You may choose to perform a much deeper assessment, but the steps below will provide a basic understanding and help improve your everyday security.

1) **Look at your home from the perspective of an adversary.** To effectively secure your home, you should examine it in the same manner and with as much detail as a sophisticated adversary would, section by section, from an outside vantage point. Many experienced criminals conduct some level of surveillance prior to committing their illegal acts, often during both daytime and nighttime.

2) **Stand on the street outside your home.** Take a good, long look and write down some notes about your initial perceptions. What stands out to you? Does your home look well-cared for, or is it in a state of disarray? Is it new or old? Does it appear to be fancy and expensive or run down? Is there trash or clutter around the outside, in the yard, or on the driveway? Owners who care for their property may have also considered their security posture and taken steps to protect their homes and loved ones. Ensure to look at your home both during the daytime and at night since your observations will be different.

3) **Security equipment.** Is there any security equipment visible as you examine the exterior of your home? This could include video monitoring equipment such as security cameras or a doorbell camera, security lighting with motion detectors, and possibly a security yard sign to suggest the presence of a security system (whether true or not).

4) **Fencing.** Is there a fence on the property? How tall is it? A short, waist-high fence does little more than mark the property line and keep little children or small pets from running into the street. A tall fence, especially if made of a solid material like wood, can restrict observation from the street and make it more difficult for a trespasser to quickly enter or exit your property without significant physical exertion. If the fence has a gate, is it closed and locked?

5) **Windows.** Can criminals easily see directly into your home? What are they able to see? This should be considered during both daytime and at night. Draperies, plantation shutters, vertical blinds, and other window coverings can limit or eliminate outside observation depending on the style chosen.

Basic Condominium or Apartment Building Security Assessment

If you live in a condominium or apartment building, consider the following points to gain a basic understanding of the security provided by your property management. You can quickly determine if the building is "loose" or if property management runs a good, tight security program. If you identify significant deficiencies, it may be valuable to have a discussion with your property management or the homeowner's association to address the concerns.

1) Guardhouse. Does your building have a guardhouse or gatehouse at the entry to the property? This may not apply if your building is located directly on the street. Is the guard-house staffed twenty-four hours per day? Are the guards alert and inquisitive? Do all guests require prearranged approval to gain access?

2) Building entry. How many doors allow entry into your building? Is each door locked with a key code or a key fob? Are all entry doors under observation by security cameras? Does the primary entrance have a doorman or a concierge who is actively paying attention to each person who comes into the building? If the doorman or concierge does not know some-one, is the guest politely and directly challenged when seeking entry? Or can an unknown individual just freely wander into the building with no concerns?

3) Security equipment. Does the building have well-main-tained security cameras in the elevators, stairwells, and possi-bly the hallways on each floor? Is any other security equipment present, such as coded door locks or ID card readers?

4) Security guards. Are members of the guard force alert and vigilant, or are they more focused on their mobile devices and what time their shifts end? Are there roving guards regularly patrolling throughout the building? Does the guard force have a high turnover, or are the guards invested in long-term employ-ment in the building? Do you know the Chief of Security? Is this person knowledgeable and actively engaged in managing the overall security posture?

5) Parking garage. If your building has a parking garage, is it well-lit and monitored by security cameras? Do security guards regularly patrol through the garage? Most garages have vehicle parking spots that are assigned to a specific unit. Is the parking spot marked with your name, a generic number, or with your specific unit number? A generic number is the best method; it is not desirable to have a direct link between your vehicle parking spot and your actual unit number or name.

Does the building require a generic vehicle sticker or rear-view mirror hang tag to be displayed with your vehicle? This is generally acceptable, but avoid displaying a sticker or hang tag that lists the name or address of the building. Otherwise, someone may see this information when your vehicle is parked out in town, and they will be able to draw a direct link between your vehicle and where you reside. If the building's current parking stickers or hang tags list this information, ask the homeowner's association to consider issuing new stickers or hang tags that do not provide any building-specific details. Your neighbors will appreciate your thoroughness.

LOOK TWICE TIP

Preserve Your Privacy

If you are new to city life, it is easy to think that no one can see into your home because you live in a high-rise condominium or apartment building, perhaps twenty or thirty floors above the ground. It is common, however, for residents in other buildings to have binoculars or very powerful telescopes to observe the spectacular city views. This equipment also allows others to watch your every movement, especially at night; some telescopes can zoom in from great distances and offer the ability to take digital pictures or video. Unless you aspire to become an "internet sensation" and world-famous overnight, you might want to close your blinds and be mindful of your activities, especially at night.

IMPROVING THE SECURITY OF YOUR HOME

After conducting a basic security assessment of your residence, it is time to address any weaknesses and make your home into a HARD POINT.

1) Review details from your home security assessment. Read over the notes you made while standing outside your home. Correct any deficiencies that were found. Fix items that are broken and manage perceptions.

LOOK TWICE TIP

Keep Your Security Preparations Secret

It is much more difficult for an assailant to conduct a successful crime or attack when they do not know what preparations you have put in place. This is true not only for your personal security but also for the security preparations you have incorporated into your home, such as what security equipment you have installed and what **standard operating procedures (SOPs)** you and your loved ones are using to defend yourselves.

Do not share information about your security preparations with others because it will only serve to degrade your advantage.

2) Clean up the exterior of your home. As noted in the **Basic Home Security Assessment** section, a clean and neat home exterior offers the outward perception that you have taken the time and attention to care for your home. Dispose of trash. Pick up toys, bicycles, and other valuables in the yard and store them in the garage or a locked storage shed behind your home. If there is no garage or storage shed behind your home, consider renting a nearby commercial storage unit. If you have a ladder stored outside your home, perhaps on the side of the garage or in your backyard, remove it. A ladder should be locked inside your garage or removed from your property; otherwise, it may be used by criminals to gain entry to your roof or upper windows, which are often left unlocked.

3) Cut shrubbery. Trim bushes and other vegetation from around your windows to eliminate hiding places for criminals trying to break into your home. Depending on your climate, another option is to plant thorny bushes below your windows, making it painful and difficult for an adversary to access your windows while also eliminating a hiding place.

4) Install security equipment. Consider installing security equipment if you do not have any devices or upgrade to new models if the existing technology is out of date. You can hire a licensed professional security company to install the equipment and provide 24/7 monitoring services, or you can install the equipment yourself. Some manufacturers provide a range of devices that can be easily self-installed at a fraction of the cost, with 24/7 monitoring also available as an option.

For the highest level of security, all of the various sensors and devices must be hard-wired to the main control unit, which is labor-intensive and expensive to install. These hard-wired systems are the most difficult for an adversary to defeat. Some very popular and widely available equipment, including do-it-yourself systems, rely on your home Wi-Fi connection to allow all of the sensors and the main control unit to communicate as necessary. There are documented cases of experienced, tech-savvy adversaries using a **Wi-Fi Deauthor** device to force this type of security equipment to disconnect from a home Wi-Fi system, providing an opportunity to break into your residence. The Wi-Fi Deauthor device acts like a jammer and prevents the equipment from functioning correctly. Other criminals may employ an actual **jammer** to block the Wi-Fi signal entirely. Although these methods are illegal, an adversary does not care since they are already planning to burglarize your home.

This is one of those times where you must weigh the POSSIBLE versus the PROBABLE. Your best choice may be to install a commercially available wireless security system and just accept the risk that an adversary might use the above methods to target your home. This may be a better option for you than not installing any security equipment if a hard-wired system is too expensive for your budget. Weigh out the variables, figure out what is POSSIBLE and what is PROBABLE, and then choose the best option for your security requirements and personal circumstances.

5) Install security lighting. Security lighting around your home is important because **more light frequently equals less crime.** Install motion detector-activated flood lights, preferably well off the ground on the second story of your home. Install an automatic porch light with a timer that turns on and off at specific times of day or has a dusk-to-dawn sensor. Criminals prefer to do their nefarious work under limited visibility conditions (meaning darkness, heavy fog, etc.) Some will go so far as to attempt to use an air rifle with BBs or pellets to quietly shoot out light bulbs prior to starting their work. **No matter where you are, use extra caution if you ever notice ALL of the lights around you are not working. The failure of the lights may have been intentional.** This applies to your home, place of work, a parking garage, or a remote section of a side street.

6) Install security fencing. Consider adding a tall, solid security fence if your home does not already have one. If your home has an existing fence, ensure it is fully serviceable, or else seek repair from a qualified professional.

7) Lock all windows. This may sound like simple advice, but it is surprising how many people leave some of their windows unlocked, especially on the second floor. If you are installing security equipment, go the extra mile and put window entry sensors on all of your second-story windows in addition to the windows on the ground floor. Some criminals will try to enter via the second story and work their way down to the ground floor inside your home.

8) Lock all entry doors. Install quality locks on all of your exterior doors, including bolt locks. If you have an attached garage, make sure to lock the door inside your garage to prevent entry to your home. This is especially important at night or when you are away from your residence. It is best to also install a bolt lock on this door for increased security. This extra protection is important in case an adversary gains access to your garage and tries to break into your home through this door. It is unlikely that your neighbors will be aware of the break-in since it is hidden within your garage, and they will not know to alert the authorities on your behalf.

Consider not lubricating the hinges on some of your squeaky doors, especially entry doors or bedroom doors. If the door squeaks, it can serve as a gentle alarm or warning that someone is approaching.

9) Install a peephole viewer privacy cover. Install a peephole privacy cover over the peephole viewer in your entry door. This is a small plastic cover that mounts inside your door over the peephole viewer. If you wish to look through the peephole viewer, the cover slides up or to the side, depending on the design. This device adds additional privacy to your entry door.

LOOK TWICE TIP

Lock Your Doors

Always keep the front door to your home LOCKED. Even better, keep all the doors to your home locked; this includes whether you are at home or away, day or night. This is a simple action to take and serves as your first line of defense. Although you may have grown up or lived in a place where people did not have to lock their doors, in the city or nearby suburbs, this is no longer an effective strategy. Many terrible crimes have occurred simply because a criminal had an "opportunity" that presented itself when someone did not lock their door(s).

10) Lock your bedroom door. When you go to sleep at night, lock your bedroom door. It only takes a second. Even though a bedroom door lock does not offer much security, it still adds one more layer of protection between you and an adversary. It lessens the chance of someone sneaking up on you while you are sleeping. If an adversary breaks through the door, you have at least bought yourself a couple of extra seconds to respond when you are abruptly awakened. That could mean the difference between life and death.

11) Seal off extra entrances. "Doggie Doors" that allow animals to freely enter and exit a home may be convenient, but they are a security threat. It is much better to remove your pet door completely, permanently seal the opening shut, and fortify your home. Do not provide an easy point of entry for an adversary to exploit.

Does a Guard Dog Live Here?

An aggressive, ferocious guard dog has a negative psychological effect on many would-be criminals. No one wants to have the powerful jaws of an angry dog clamp down on their arm or leg. **The mere appearance of a guard dog living in your home, real or perceived, may encourage criminals to think twice and choose a different target.** You may love animals and want to have a guard dog live with you. Or you might choose to just give the appearance of a guard dog living in your home. Post "Beware of Dog" signs in a few visible locations around your property, such as on a fence gate. Put a large dog bowl on your porch or patio filled with water or dry dog food. Place a big synthetic bone dog chew in a visible location on a walkway or driveway. These visual signs may lead a criminal to believe a dog lives in your home and then choose a different target. Shape perception to your advantage.

12) Keep your garage door closed. Whenever you are not outside in the vicinity of your garage, close and lock your garage door. Consider installing an automatic garage door opener since this will prevent your garage door from being manually opened by force unless activated by a remote control or mechanically disengaged from inside the garage. In some areas of the country, it can get incredibly hot inside a garage in the warmer months. Some people in these areas are surprised when they leave their garage door open unattended for hours and later find out that thieves have stolen valuable yard equipment or other items stored inside the garage. In some areas, including the suburbs, criminals will drive through a neighborhood looking for open garage doors. A couple of thieves will rush up to the house, grab any items of value they see in the garage, run back to the waiting vehicle, and then quickly depart. These "smash and grab" crimes are easily prevented. Lock up what you do not want to have stolen, and keep valuables out of sight.

13) Lock all vehicles. If you have the space, store your vehicles in your garage each night. Ensure to lock your vehicles, even in the garage with the garage door closed; this includes both automobiles and motorcycles and serves as an extra layer of security. Also, lock your vehicles when parked in the driveway or in the street along the curb. Ensure you do not leave any valuables or papers visible through your car windows from outside your car. If criminals see an item of value, such as a laptop or a briefcase, on one of your car seats, you might find a broken window and the item missing when you return to your vehicle. Instead, put the items into the car trunk out of view, or even better, bring the items with you into your home.

14) Hidden spare key. Do you have a spare key hidden outside of your home in case of an emergency or to allow a loved one to gain entry if they are accidentally locked out? Many people do. Criminals know this and will quickly search through all of the usual "secret" locations where you are likely to hide a key. Do not be fooled; criminals are experts at finding your hidden key. Instead, consider putting your key in a small waterproof key container or a watertight bag and then bury the key three to four inches underground in a nondescript location. You can bury the key in a flower bed, perhaps in your backyard, out of view of the street. Note the color of the soil or any wood chips as you complete the task so that your hidden key location looks the same as the surrounding ground and does not draw attention. It may be harder to access the key, but it will remain safe until you need it in an emergency.

Instead of hiding the extra key, it can also be stored in either a portable or permanently mounted **key storage safe**. This is a small, extremely strong lock box that is opened with a pushbutton code or spin dial. You may be familiar with the portable version often used by realtors to allow authorized entry to other realtors showing a home to a client.

Another technique is to **install a keyless security lock** on a door to your home that uses a push-button keypad to enter a combination without any physical key. The latest technology goes one step further than a physical combination and instead allows you to electronically share your encrypted key combination with the lock through a simple tap from your smartphone or smartwatch. The lock opens quickly while your combination remains securely stored within your smart device.

15) Your home is your temple. In general, Americans are by nature open, friendly, and welcoming people compared to some other cultures around the world. Our good-hearted, welcoming nature and willingness to quickly open our homes to people we do not know well can be exploited by those who wish to do us harm. **As a general rule, your home is a special place that should be reserved for your closest friends and family.** Do not invite anyone into your home or private living space unless you know them well and they are part of your "inner circle" of friends and family. If you want to bring someone into your home briefly, ensure they remain in the "public" area of your home. Do not invite them into a bedroom, home office, or other "non-public" areas of your home. Visitors or workers who you do not know well may visually case your home while inside, looking for any visible items of value. In some situations, it is difficult to prevent workers from entering private parts of your residence. The goal is to limit how often this happens and reduce visitors to close friends and family.

STAY SAFE

The Cable Guy

An elderly couple moved into their new home and arranged to have cable service installed. The cable installer arrived a few days later and set up their service on several televisions in the home. As a retired law enforcement officer, the husband noticed the cable installer was paying very close attention to the items in their home as he freely moved about completing his work.

Two days later, in the middle of the night, three men broke into the home while the elderly couple slept in a nearby bedroom. The men quickly grabbed several high-value items and departed the home without further incident. Neither the husband nor the wife were harmed, but both were shaken up by the burglary and just how close the criminals got to them while they were sleeping.

The next morning, the husband filed a police report and called the cable company to mention the situation and inquire about the cable installer. The cable company noted that the installer had called in and quit the day before. Although the installer may or may not have been one of the three men who broke into the home, it was likely that he had at least tipped off some of his associates.

CHECKLIST FOR SAFE AT HOME

___ Review details from your home security assessment and correct any deficiencies.

___ Clean up the exterior of your home. Dispose of trash. Pick up toys, bicycles, ladders, and other valuables in the yard and store them in the garage, a locked storage shed, or a rented commercial storage unit located near your residence.

___ Trim bushes and other vegetation away from in front of windows.

___ Install security equipment.

___ Install security lighting.

___ Install security fencing.

___ Lock all windows, including upper floors.

___ Lock all entry doors.

___ Install a peephole viewer privacy cover in your entry door.

___ Lock your bedroom door when you go to sleep at night.

___ Seal off extra entrances such as "Doggie Doors."

___ Keep your garage door closed and locked when not in the immediate vicinity.

___ Lock all vehicles overnight, including those inside your garage, in the driveway, or parked in the street along the curb. Ensure you do not leave any valuables or papers in your vehicle that are visible from the outside.

___ Be cautious about hiding a spare key outside your home. Instead, consider installing a key storage safe or keyless security lock.

___ Limit who visits your home to close friends and family. For other visitors, keep them in the "public" area of your home as much as possible.

PART 4

SAFE AT WORK

ASSESSING YOUR WORKPLACE

Work is an important part of most people's lives, and many spend a substantial amount of time in the workplace each week. Although some people now have the opportunity to work from home or in a hybrid role where they only go into the workplace a few days per week, many others are still required to show up at their place of work every day. This may be five or even six days each week, depending on the job.

Considering the amount of time spent at work, it is prudent to conduct a basic security assessment of your workplace and gain an understanding of the overall security posture provided by your employer. Are you relatively safe, or is security lacking and nothing more than an afterthought? Quietly and privately observe the following points in your workplace at your convenience to build a deeper understanding of the security environment you face each day. Consider the security of the building where you work, as well as your specific office or workspace within the building. These are general guidelines and will vary significantly based on your particular situation, but they should allow you to get a "feel" for the type of security measures that are in place.

Assessing the Employer:

1) **Type of industry.** What do you do for a living? Do you work in a factory that makes children's toys? Or are you involved in the sale and distribution of legal medical marijuana? These two industries will have very different security profiles; the children's toy industry does not tend to attract desperate individuals the way some other industries might. Do you work in a law firm focused on estate planning in a high-rise business tower, or are you working alone overnight in a twenty-four-hour convenience store located on a rough corner in the city? These different occupations and environments will require different security protocols to ensure the protection of employees. **Knowing your type of industry provides the bedrock for understanding what security challenges may lie ahead.**

2) **Size of firm.** What is the size of your employer at your daily work location? You may work for a huge, nationally known firm with tens of thousands of employees, but your focus is on the place where you physically go to work each day. If the company is headquartered in Los Angeles but you work at a small ten-person office in Indianapolis, we want to focus on your local security profile in Indiana. With this understanding and considering where you work each day, how large is the firm? Is it a family-sized operation, such as a dry cleaner or a small shop or bistro? Is your employer a medium-sized company with 300 employees on-site in a high-rise building spread over multiple floors? Or are you employed in a large location such as a factory or a stand-alone building or complex with several thousand employees? **There will be distinct security expectations for each of these different situations.**

3) Workplace culture. What is your workplace culture? This may be affected a great deal by the size of your workplace. Does the culture feel like a family where everyone knows each other well and where there is very little turnover of employees? Or is there a significant employee turnover rate, and many people know little to nothing about their fellow workers? Can you count on others in your workplace if there is a problem, or do you not even know their names and have no personal connection? Are employees committed to the company, or is the work environment "just a job" and transitory? **Employees who are committed to their work and have caring, connected relationships with each other tend to be more aware of any concerns in the workplace, often in advance of any actual trouble. They also tend to feel more included and consider themselves "part of the team." This may lead to a more resilient and secure environment.**

4) Frequency of outsiders visiting the workplace. There are different expectations for various types of businesses regarding contact with outsiders who are not employees. If you work in retail, store patrons are the lifeblood of your company, and there will be a steady flow of customers in and out of the store throughout business hours. Some businesses, however, do not have much contact with outsiders. If you work in an office setting for a company that provides a service, such as an accounting or legal firm, visits may be by appointment only and more limited in number. Some other service providers, including tradesmen, generally go to customers' homes to work and have few, if any, visitors at their company office. With the exception of a delivery person, anyone else who shows up at the office would be unusual and potentially a security concern. **Security tends to be easier to control if the identity and purpose of each visitor are known in advance due to an appointment**

or an ongoing relationship or if there is no expectation for any visitors of any type on-site. For many businesses, this is not possible and will be an ongoing security challenge that must be closely monitored.

Assessing the Facility:

5) Building entry procedures. How many doors allow entry into your building? There may be multiple emergency exits, but entry may be limited to one or two doors, depending on the building structure. Are there any controls on entry? Are all employees required to wear an identification card with a current photo visibly displayed? Do all visitors have to sign in and have an escort take them to their appointment? Are entry doors to individual businesses constantly locked and require a unique key code or a key fob to gain entry? If a person is not positively known to security, is that person challenged upon seeking entry? Or can an unknown individual freely wander into the building unchallenged and with no concerns? Are the entry doors to the building locked after normal working hours?

6) Security equipment. Does the building have well-maintained security cameras near the entrance, in the elevators, stairwells, and the hallways on each floor? Identify if the security team monitors all security camera coverage around the perimeter of the building and at key points within the facility so they can effectively monitor who is going where and what activities are happening in the building. Are emergency exit doors alarmed if opened? Are the elevators coded to only go to a specific floor based on an individual's appointment? Are duress buttons installed and working properly at key locations around the facility in case of trouble, especially in a parking garage or parking lot? Each duress button should initiate a visual and auditory alarm when activated.

7) Security guards. Are security guards present? Is there one guard per shift or an entire team? Are the guards armed with firearms, or do they only have radios? Are the members of the guard force alert and vigilant? Do all guards remain at a fixed point, perhaps in the lobby or near the primary entrance? Are there additional roving guards who regularly patrol throughout the facility? Does the guard force have a high turnover rate, or are the guards invested in long-term employment in the building? Do you know the Chief of Security? Is this person visible on-site and actively engaged in managing the overall security posture? Ensure to meet the security guards with whom you come into contact and greet them each day when you see them. Become known to them and build mutual respect.

8) Parking garage. If the building has a parking garage, is it well-lit and monitored by security cameras? Do security guards regularly patrol through the garage? If multiple businesses lease space in the building, the garage may have vehicle parking spots that are reserved in a block for a specific business or with individual generic numbers. It is best to avoid having a parking spot marked with either your title or your actual name since it is not desirable to have a direct link between any vehicle parking spot and a specific person. Does the building also require a generic vehicle sticker or rear-view mirror hang tag to be displayed on or inside each vehicle? This is generally acceptable as long as the name and address of the building or facility are not listed. Instead, the company should use some type of generic symbol with a corresponding number. The logic behind this is to avoid having someone see a sticker or hang tag identifying your place of work when your vehicle is parked out in the city, allowing them to draw a link between your vehicle and where you work. Although a parking garage is superior to parking on the street since it may have some security protections, it obviously will not provide complete vehicle protection like a private home garage that is fully enclosed. Your automobile may still be accessible to other employees and possibly visitors or workers who park in close proximity to you. It is often surprising how many visitors or workers pass through a parking garage each day for a multitude of reasons. Do you feel safe while walking to your vehicle in the parking garage, especially after normal working hours?

9) Parking lot. Does your workplace have a parking lot instead of a parking garage? Many of the same questions apply, along with a few more. Is there a tall security fence (approximately six to seven feet high, likely with barbed wire along the top) around the parking lot with a gatehouse and security guard controlling the point of entry? Is the security guard paying attention to all activities in the parking lot, or is their focus elsewhere? Observe the lighting to ensure it is adequate at night. Do you feel comfortable returning to your vehicle at any time of day by yourself? If not, walk with others who are departing the workplace at the same time or ask someone to accompany you to your vehicle for extra safety, especially at night or after normal working hours.

10) Additional facilities. This may include an on-site fitness center, cafeteria, or daycare facility. Look for security camera coverage at entrances and key locations in the facilities. Does entry into each location require the presentation of a security credential, such as an identification card with a current photo and a proximity chip or a key card/key fob? It is important that physical access is granted only to individuals who have an appropriate security credential and a reason to be in the facility. Otherwise, access should be denied. By requiring a security credential to gain access, an electronic audit trail is created that provides a historical record of who accessed which facility and at what time. Audit trails can provide essential data should an investigation be required at a later time.

WHAT TO DO, WHAT NOT TO DO

A Safe Workplace

Sergio wanted to apply his new knowledge and privately conduct a basic security assessment of his workplace to gain peace of mind. He decided that he would observe the security posture little by little over a few days as he went about his daily routine so as not to draw any attention or cause concern. As he approached the mid-rise office building where he worked, Sergio noted discreetly mounted security cameras well out of reach above the first floor on the outside of the building. The cameras appeared to cover the length of the building, with some cameras focused on the primary entrance to the building. As he walked into the building through the main doors, he noted strong **electromagnetic locks** (also known as magnetic locks) mounted at the top of each entry door. Sergio had learned that these locks often had a holding force of up to 1200 pounds when activated and would very effectively hold the perimeter doors closed on the front of the building. He observed that the building had a small sign on the glass entry doors that listed the building hours; the building was open for business from 7:00 a.m. to 6:30 p.m. Sergio knew that people could keep working in their offices as late as they wished, but the entrance doors were locked at 6:30 p.m. He was glad to know this policy was in place since it would eliminate the chance of any outsiders just wandering into the building at night unless they had a reason to be there.

Sergio entered the lobby, ensuring he had his building identification card with his photograph visibly displayed and clipped to his neck lanyard hanging on the outside of his coat. He noticed two uniformed security guards watching everyone who came into the lobby, and a third guard was examining a guest's ID and helping the person to enter their personal information into the visitor's log. One of the security guards greeted Sergio with a friendly "Good Morning!" as he glanced at the ID card hanging on Sergio's neck lanyard. Sergio presented his identification card to the ID card reader at the narrow access gate. The proximity chip in Sergio's identification card confirmed his identity, and the access gate opened briefly to allow entry.

Sergio continued to the elevator bank and presented his identification card to the elevator control panel; it instantly read what floor he worked on and directed him to a specific elevator that took him directly to his work floor. He greeted the security guard who was standing nearby, closely watching over the area. As Sergio walked toward the elevator, he observed a discreet security camera in the corner of the elevator bank's ceiling, which monitored everyone's movements.

Sergio arrived on the fifth floor, and as he exited the elevator, he noted that a security camera was also present in the elevator. He continued down the hall and presented his identification card to a reader on the wall next to the glass entry doors that controlled access to his workplace. His identification card validated his approved access with an audible chirp, and the electromagnetic lock that held the door shut released its powerful grip for a few seconds. An audit trail was created in the badging system showing that Sergio had arrived at work at 8:28 a.m.

Over the next few days, Sergio continued to observe various security features as he went about his day in the building. He noticed the location of security cameras that he had never previously paid attention to. On a few occasions, he saw a uniformed security guard quietly patrolling the hallway outside of his company workspace. He paid closer attention to the security elements in place in the parking garage and felt comfortable going to his car at any hour of the day. He also noted a security presence in and around the building cafeteria on the few occasions when he went to purchase some food. Sergio was confident that the building management provided a safe and comfortable environment where he could work with few security concerns.

WHAT TO DO, WHAT NOT TO DO:

This example demonstrates what conducting a basic security assessment of your workplace might look like in practice, including what to observe as you move about the building during the workday. Be discrete while examining the security posture of your workplace. You do not want to draw attention; avoid giving the appearance that you are casing the workplace or planning some type of nefarious activity. Just remain observant as you go through each workday, collecting little bits of information about the security posture over several days. Over a short period of time, you will develop a fairly accurate picture of whether your workplace is safe and secure or just a problem waiting to happen.

LOOK TWICE TIP

Keep the Lights On

If you are concerned that a stalker or another adversary may be watching your place of work at night, **keep all of the lights turned on in your office space or throughout your entire work floor during hours of darkness.** By using this technique, an adversary will not be able to observe which office light is turned on shortly after you enter the building, which hinders their ability to identify your specific office. If an adversary already knows which office is yours, they will not be able to observe your office light turn off and then be ready to take immediate action as you exit from the building. Furthermore, this technique will allow you to effectively conceal your movements within the building from outside observation during hours of darkness. Keep in mind that for this technique to work, the windows must be covered by blinds or curtains that only allow the transmission of light to be visible from the street.

CHECKLIST FOR ASSESSING YOUR WORKPLACE

__ Type of industry
__ Size of firm
__ Workplace culture
__ Frequency of outsiders visiting the workplace
__ Building entry procedures
__ Security equipment
__ Security guards
__ Parking garage
__ Parking lot
__ Additional facilities (fitness center, cafeteria, daycare facility)

WORKPLACE VIOLENCE

The workplace is one of the few locations where most people must go on a daily basis. Considering how much time most people spend at work each day and the number of angry people in society, it is an unfortunate reality that **workplace violence** is a significant concern. Government agencies and other experts have written a large body of information on this topic that is broadly available in the public domain. The goal of this section is not to reinvent the wheel when it comes to dealing with workplace violence. Instead, some strategies and concepts are offered that may prove effective in how you prepare for and handle any workplace violence issues to enhance your everyday security.

Workplace violence can happen suddenly and stem from many different root causes. If your company poorly handles an **employee termination**, it can potentially lead to workplace violence. An employee termination must be carefully scripted and prepared for in advance by human resources (HR) and security personnel working closely together. HR and security personnel often have had special training on best practices for employee terminations and may have years of experience under their belts. Whenever possible, these terminations should be handled with dignity, off-site and away from other employees, concluding with the employee returning all security credentials (IDs, key fobs, etc.) and then being respectfully led off of the premises. All security personnel should be aware of the termination and that the former employee is not allowed back on the premises for any reason. Former employees should be provided with contact information should they need to call or email concerning any outstanding issues, but they must also be advised that they are no longer allowed to return to the worksite. A terminated employee attempting to return to the workplace after the fact should be viewed as a threat until further investigation.

Workplace violence can also stem from inappropriate behavior or a disagreement that spirals out of control between employees at the worksite. **PROBLEMATIC EMPLOYEES** are generally well-known among their co-workers as troubled individuals with a poor reputation in the office; few workers are surprised when they hear who was involved in a situation after the fact. Co-workers will often say, "It was just a matter of time," or a similar comment after an incident occurs. HR and security may have received complaints or concerns about a problematic employee in the past, but there likely was not enough derogatory information to take conclusive action until the proverbial "pot boils over." You need to be aware of who these individuals are in your work setting and limit your contact as much as possible. It is essential to report any incidents or concerning details to HR or security, no matter how small, so that a complete track record and detailed file can be established. Without this history, company leadership will be poorly positioned to take action and remove the problematic employee from the workplace prior to a full-blown incident.

Unless effective security protocols are in place and consistently enforced, an **UNWELCOME VISITOR** may find their way into the workplace with bad intentions that could quickly escalate into a violent encounter. Unwelcome visitors might include stalkers, unwanted suitors, angry or jilted former or current boyfriends, girlfriends, or spouses. Knowing that you or one of your loved ones can usually be found during standard working hours at the workplace, an unwelcome visitor may view your place of employment as an effective place to confront you and possibly cause embarrassment or worse in front of co-workers. The unwelcome visitor may initially say he "just wants to talk" with the target of his attention, but the desire to communicate may not be shared by both parties, and the situation quickly degrades. Businesses are seeing an increasing number of unwelcome visitors show up unannounced at the workplace to confront their domestic partners, and some of these situations quickly spiral out of control, resulting in violence that affects other innocent bystanders.

Remember you want to **AVOID, AVOID, AVOID.** The best way to deal with this kind of situation is to prevent the circumstances from ever happening by controlling visitors and preventing them from entering the premises unless their identity and clear purpose are known in advance of their arrival. It is your responsibility to know what your company's security representatives expect you to do in a potential workplace violence situation. Listen to their guidance, know what actions you should take, and have a clear understanding of where you should go. If you have not received any training, request that your company leadership provide a class to teach you and other employees what to do in your workplace.

WHAT TO DO, WHAT NOT TO DO

Trouble Comes to the Store

A large, nationally known company had a problem. At one of their local retail stores in a major southern city, the store manager reported an **UNWELCOME VISITOR** had stopped by the previous evening. The visitor had just been released from state prison and was a member of a well-known violent gang with chapters in cities across the United States.

One of the store's employees was the girlfriend of the unwelcome visitor and also the mother of his child from before his confinement. While her boyfriend was serving his sentence in state prison, she was secretly having intimate relations with another employee who worked in the retail store. Following his release from prison, the unwelcome visitor became aware of the affair and proclaimed that he intended to kill his girlfriend's new partner.

Both employees in the store were valuable, long-time members of the sales team and well-liked by the manager and other employees. Their secret relationship had remained unknown to their colleagues until the unwelcome visitor made his first appearance. The unwelcome visitor came into the store just before closing, looking for his girlfriend's new suitor; fortunately, the man was not in the store that evening. The other employees were extremely frightened by the unwelcome visitor's sudden appearance, violent demeanor, and ominous message.

The store manager immediately contacted corporate security personnel at the company's national headquarters, located far away in a different part of the country. Corporate security leadership alerted law enforcement and hired a private, heavily armed plainclothes protective officer to remain in the store until the situation calmed down and the threat receded. Based on the unwelcome visitor's violent history, there was significant concern that he would return to make good on his threats. Law enforcement was also concerned but lacked the resources to do anything other than check in with store management once or twice a day during business hours.

This situation had a devastating effect on the other employees. Several quit their jobs outright and went home immediately, afraid to return to work and not wanting any further involvement in the continuing drama. Based on guidance from the protective officer, the store manager asked the male suitor to go home and stay away from the store until the situation was resolved. The girlfriend continued to work but was visibly upset and scared. The saga put the entire store on edge, pending any final resolution.

WHAT TO DO, WHAT NOT TO DO:

The unwelcome visitor did not return, possibly due to corporate security getting ahead of the problem by hiring a highly trained protective officer. The protective officer's presence visibly changed the security profile of the small retail store and transformed it into more of a **HARD TARGET**. The removal of the male suitor also helped to defuse the situation and separate the drama from the workplace.

This scenario demonstrates how the private actions of two employees, although consenting adults on their own time well away from the workplace, can still invite significant trouble that affects the entire workforce in the form of an **UNWELCOME VISITOR.**

PREPARING IN ADVANCE

Some work environments do not have a formal security staff or presence to provide advice, possibly because the company is too small or the budget does not allow much money for security. In these situations, it is important to think ahead about what steps you would take to protect yourself if a situation degraded into workplace violence. Use the easy-to-remember concept taught by numerous government agencies: **RUN, HIDE, FIGHT.** If a situation turns violent, **RUN** away. This means you must **GET OFF THE X** and leave the situation immediately; put distance between you and the violence. Get out of the office, depart the building, and move to a safe place. If you are already removed from the "X" where the incident is occurring but cannot leave the workplace to get to a safe place, then **HIDE**. If the violence comes to you and you can no longer **HIDE**, then you must **FIGHT**, like your life depends on it—because it does.

PREPARE IN ADVANCE to help you succeed and live in case you have to face this situation for real someday. Below are a few steps to help you prepare.

1) Memorize the layout of your workplace. You need to know your way around both with the lights on and in the dark in case you are in the office after hours and the lights are cut off.

2) If you are able to RUN, plan a location where you will go. Will you head to a stairwell to escape the building? If you can exit the building quickly and get outside, where will you go? Look around outside your facility and plan ahead for a location where you can fully escape from any violence. Can you get into another building down the street where you will be safe? Where will you go if the situation happens after normal work hours? If unsure of where to go, keep running until you are well away from the situation. Ensure you are fully out of view and behind something solid, like a building or a thick wall that can protect you from possible gunfire. Get as low as possible to the ground to minimize your exposure. Call for help and remain on the phone.

3) Identify all exits, including multiple routes to get to each exit. There may only be one pathway to each exit, depending on the size of the workplace.

4) Locate places where you can HIDE. This is like playing a really serious game of Hide and Seek. Find excellent hiding places in advance while you have the time and when you are calm and thinking clearly. You might need to use one of these locations as a hiding place to save your life, so prepare accordingly.

5) If you have to FIGHT, fully commit. You will have to muster the maximum intensity of which you are capable and **FIGHT** with every ounce of your spirit. Use EXTREME VIOLENCE and objects nearby as weapons to defeat your adversary. This is a last resort, and although you may not want to be in this situation, it is now where you are. It is YOU versus YOUR ADVERSARY. Fight like your life depends on it so you can go home to your loved ones afterward.

LOOK TWICE TIP

Use Caution With Doorways

A doorway is often referred to in the security world as a **FUNNEL OF DEATH.** To enter or exit a room, you must pass through a narrow doorway which serves as a **CHOKEPOINT**. An armed adversary can readily control a doorway and cause great harm to you or anyone else trying to enter or exit. A doorway is one of the most likely places where you could be killed.

Do not linger around doorways or move through slowly. If you must pass through, do so deliberately with explosive speed and move well away from the opening. Avoid doorways whenever possible.

For additional resources and videos concerning workplace violence, you are encouraged to consult the official US Government websites:

Department of Homeland Security (DHS) www.dhs.gov
Federal Bureau of Investigation (FBI) www.fbi.gov

CHECKLIST FOR PREPARING IN ADVANCE

___ Memorize the layout of your workplace, both with the lights on and in the dark.

___ In case a situation turns violent, plan a location where you will go in case you are able to **RUN.**

___ Identify all exits along with multiple routes to get to each exit.

___ Locate places where you can **HIDE.** Do this in advance while you have time and when you are calm and thinking clearly.

___ If you have to **FIGHT,** fully commit. It is **YOU versus YOUR ADVERSARY.** Fight like your life depends on it so you can go home to your loved ones later.

TARGETED AT WORK

As mentioned earlier in this chapter, you probably go to your place of work a minimum of several days per week. Along with your home, this makes your workplace one of the most likely places where an adversary can locate you on a regular basis. You may be "targeted" or "picked up" for observation or interdiction while arriving at your place of employment, stepping out for lunch, or departing from work for the day.

If you are like most people, you unwittingly keep a fairly regular schedule unless you intentionally focus on your life patterns and seek to alter your habits. Your patterns will quickly become visible and predictable to a keen observer. Your work schedule and patterns associated with the workplace may offer an adversary a window to gain access to you, either visually or physically. Keep this in the back of your mind and stay aware.

Is Someone Following You?

If you have concerns that you may be followed by a stalker, an aggressive business competitor, or some other type of adversary, pay close attention when you are departing from work, home, or any location where you leave on a predictable schedule. Work diligently to **AVOID PATTERNS** whenever possible.

Using your rearview and side view mirrors on your car, watch to see if another vehicle pulls out shortly after you leave the parking garage or parking lot where you park your vehicle during the workday. If you observe someone pulling out at roughly the same time as your vehicle, gather as much data as you can without giving away the fact that you are observing this individual. Do not let them see you staring into your mirrors, and do not turn your head to get a better look. This may alert your adversary that they have been "burned" (spotted), and they may stop following you temporarily until another time of their choosing when you do not see them. You do not want to let them know that you are aware of their presence. Sunglasses can assist you and help to conceal your eye movements during the daytime. Also, be aware that the person watching you may not be behind you; instead, they may actually be "leading you" and might pull out in front of your vehicle down the block once they see you exit the parking garage or lot. You must remain aware of what is going around your vehicle in all directions (360 degrees).

If you identify someone watching you, it is important to collect as much data as you can. Mentally identify key details such as the license plate number and state of issuance, vehicle make, model, and color, and if there are any significant attributes to the car that are noteworthy or difficult to change quickly. License plates can be switched rapidly if mounted with magnets, but it is not possible to rapidly remove a large dent in the front quarter panel or the bumper or quickly cover a major scrape on a car door. Does the vehicle have any unusual customization, such as unique tires or wheels? Is there any distinctive writing or large stickers on the vehicle? Were you able to see the occupant(s)? Were they male or female, and how many? Were there any distinguishing characteristics to their appearance?

Keep a small spiral notebook with a push-button ball-point pen handy in your car. Place the notebook on your leg and take notes (safely!) as you drive. This technique becomes much easier with practice and is especially useful for recording the license plate number or other details that may quickly slip from memory. When viewing license plate numbers in your vehicle's rearview mirror, the numbers will appear backward. You will have to mentally decipher them into the correct license plate number before writing them in the notebook.

PART 5

OUT IN TOWN

OVERVIEW

You are likely to spend the bulk of your time in one of three locations: at home, in your workplace, and out in town. This chapter will examine the specifics of certain locations and types of events that you may encounter while out in town in order to provide you with the everyday security knowledge you need to navigate the urban jungle safely and successfully.

When you are at home or in your workplace, you tend to be in a **HARD POINT** where your security situation is relatively clear, and you have had the opportunity to make advance preparations in case something happens. This offers you a security advantage. However, when you are out on the streets running errands, shopping, exercising in the park, or attending a large sporting event, the situation around you will be much more fluid. These everyday environments have a lot of unknown variables, and the security situation can degrade quickly; furthermore, it is unlikely that you will have the benefit of extensive preparation. You are most vulnerable when you are on the street or at other venues between HARD POINTS.

You have to live your life, and if you are like most people, staying couped up in your home or workplace all the time is neither desirable nor a viable life option. That said, if you live in a violent or dangerous area, it is essential to **minimize your exposure** or the time that an adversary is able to "get at you" outside of a HARD POINT. This is an ongoing balancing act that only you will be able to manage appropriately.

PERSONAL SPACE

There are a few ideas you should keep in mind as you go about your day out in town. One is the concept of **PERSONAL SPACE**. Visualize an imaginary circular force field that extends out about three feet (a yard) from your body in all directions. This is the minimum distance for your personal space; a greater distance is even better. It is important to maintain this personal space from others as a safety buffer. Obviously, this is not always possible. In some circumstances, such as walking on a crowded city sidewalk or while riding in mass transit, such as a subway car during rush hour, other people will be pressed up against you or inside your personal space. Whenever you can, however, try to avoid having anyone whom you do not know well linger within this personal space—they are too close to you.

When someone gets this close, it is common to start feeling somewhat uncomfortable. This is a natural concern, and the uneasy feeling alerts you to promptly make adjustments as necessary to increase your security. Keeping this minimal distance provides some room to react and lessens the chances of being groped in a crowded setting, having someone drop something into your pocket for an evil purpose (such as drugs or a small GPS tracking device), or a pickpocket taking something out of your pocket such as your wallet. In extreme circumstances, it may lessen the chances of you being easily stabbed without warning.

Be aware that the concept of personal space varies a bit between cultures. Some cultures are more comfortable standing or moving in close proximity, and although it may feel awkward to many Americans, it could just be a product of the other person's upbringing and culture. Stay aware.

WHAT TO DO, WHAT NOT TO DO

Approached by the Cult

A mom was in a grocery store parking lot with her eight-year-old son. She had just parked her car and was leading her son into the store to purchase some groceries for the week. Without warning, two members of a well-known cult approached briskly and moved very close to the mom and her son. They identified themselves as members of the controversial religious group and aggressively began pressuring the mother to listen to their message. The mother had heard stories about the cult actively recruiting in the area and was frightened by their overly aggressive demeanor and pushy approach; their full intentions were not clear, and she was alarmed. They were violating her **PERSONAL SPACE** and were standing far too close to her and her young son.

The woman was fearful of the two men, and she did not know where the conversation was headed. Like any mom, she wanted to ensure the safety of her son at all costs. Moving backward a few feet, the mom extended her arm and put her hand up straight in front of both men, telling them in a loud, clear voice to step back and leave her and her son alone. She immediately canceled her shopping plans, jumped back into her car with her son, locked the car doors, and smoothly drove away from the parking lot. The men did not attempt to pursue her as she moved back to her car, nor did they try to follow her as she departed the area in her vehicle. We call this **BREAKING CONTACT**. The mother and her son returned home without incident, and she contacted family and a close friend to tell them about this uncomfortable situation.

WHAT TO DO, WHAT NOT TO DO:

The mom intuitively sensed something was wrong based on the demeanor of the two men and how they violated her **PERSONAL SPACE**. She chose to immediately **BREAK CONTACT**, putting distance between the aggressors and her and her son. She also sent a clear physical signal and verbal command telling the two men to leave her alone. As soon as she got into the car, the mom locked all the vehicle doors, which delayed any quick follow-up response from the two men and added a physical barrier. She drove away smoothly and in full control of the vehicle so that she did not hit an object or another person in the parking lot while upset and trying to put distance between her car and the two men.

After arriving home, the mother reported the situation to trusted family and friends, sharing important details for later reflection. The mom chose a good course of action for handling this situation since she did not know the intentions of the two aggressive men. If you face a similar situation, take the same actions to keep you and your loved ones safe.

AWARENESS AND PROFILING

Whenever you are out in town, **maintain a sense of awareness** no matter what you are doing or where you are located. Be aware of who is around you at all times. Pay special attention to those who are located closest to you, but also look ten or twenty feet away to see others who are just beyond your immediate proximity. **"Keep your head on a swivel"** is a common saying among security professionals. This means keeping your head up and smoothly shifting your gaze from side to side, ensuring that you are fully taking in the environment around you. Is someone watching you move through a store or walk down the street? Is this person paying far too much attention to what you or your children are doing? If so, it is worth monitoring closely. Keep aware of your surroundings and any changing circumstances. Stay alert and be ready.

The next time you go to a large public area where there are a lot of people, move off to the side and watch the crowd for a few moments. You can learn a lot by seeing how people act and carry themselves. Some people will be fully aware and focused, as we just discussed. Many others will have no clue about what is going on around them. They are completely focused on the screen of their mobile device, oblivious to who is near them, who is watching them, and what dangers may lie just ahead. It is amazing to see this same phenomenon occur at night when security threats are even higher. To make matters worse, you will see some people wearing headphones or earbuds, completely removing their ability to hear sounds from the local environment and further isolating their senses and overall awareness. It is not surprising that criminals observe these same people who are completely engrossed in their phones and judge them to be easy targets. **Put your mobile device away, take out the earbuds, and pay attention to the environment around you.** It is your choice.

PROFILING WORKS. Many people have been told countless times over the years that profiling is not effective, but this is simply not true. There is a reason our most critical federal security services spend so much time on profiling in order to keep our citizens safe when it really matters. When you are out in town and maintaining a high level of awareness, stay alert for signs that someone may be about to commit a criminal act or harm you. If a person is wearing a "hoodie" (a hooded sweatshirt) with the hood up and drawn closely around their head as if to hide their identity, it is **PROBABLE** that they are doing just that—they are trying to hide their identity. This is a bad sign, especially if the person is moving quickly or aggressively toward you. If they also are wearing a face mask (such as a surgical mask used to protect against airborne viruses), you can add this to the profile, and it becomes even more **PROBABLE** that this person is trying to conceal their identity and is potentially looking for a target to exploit. If the person appears agitated or nervous, add these details to further refine the quick profile you are building. All of these observations add up to a **DEMEANOR HIT**. You are seeing enough details based on the person's outward behavior to confidently make a decision about their likely intent or desired course of action. Modify your behavior accordingly.

If you see a concealed firearm or weapon **PRINTING** through the person's clothing, meaning that you can see the outline of the concealed weapon, although it is covered by the individual's clothing, this is another detail we can add to our profile. Keep in mind that the individual may be legally licensed by state authorities to carry a concealed weapon, or the person could be a member of law enforcement, but this detail needs to be considered as a part of your quick profile.

Is the person acting or moving alone or working with others as part of a team? Is the individual part of a group of young people hanging out along a street where you need to pass on foot? Is the group just bored and passing the time? Or are they actively harassing those who pass by? Sometimes, groups of young people are just hanging out and enjoying each other's company. Other times, they may be waiting for something exciting to happen to break the boredom. In the worst case, the group is menacing or harming those who pass by. If you feel uncomfortable and the **PROFILE** of an individual or group points to a high **PROBABILITY** that bad things are about to happen, it is likely your intuition telling you that a problem is brewing. **Recognize the DEMEANOR HIT and quickly BREAK CONTACT. Move to a HARD POINT and seek assistance.** As a wise person once said, "If it looks like a pear, smells like a pear, and tastes like a pear, what is it? It is probably a pear."

WHAT TO DO, WHAT NOT TO DO
Heading Back to the Hotel Alone

In a major city in the Deep South, a businessman was finally wrapping up a long day at the national sales conference he was attending for the week. He had never been to this city before and missed his family back up North. The business-man's hotel was only a few blocks from the conference center, and **he decided he would walk back alone** prior to going out for a late dinner and calling his family.

Not used to the sweltering heat, he loosened his tie and took off his suitcoat as he walked along a major secondary road. He appeared to be uncomfortable as he fumbled with his heavy leather messenger bag which was overflowing with materials he received during the conference. Juggling his suitcoat and bag, the man was able to find his mobile phone and sent a quick text to his wife and kids. He looked around, briefly confused about where to turn, and decided to take what looked like a shortcut via a quiet side road toward his hotel.

With his attention focused on the weight of his messen-ger bag and responding to texts on his phone, the business-man failed to notice the man who was walking behind him along the sidewalk. The man was about twenty yards back, and he visibly nodded as a signal to the other three men, one on each corner of the upcoming intersection. The other three men watched closely as the businessman walked by with his **head down and focused on his phone**, unaware of their presence. They noted his suit, which was unusual in the summer heat, and instantly **knew he was from out of town**. These men saw conference attendees all the time and knew he would be an easy target. To their eyes, this man appeared to be a wealthy "mark."

The businessman turned from the sidewalk of the sec-ondary road onto a quiet side road that wound behind the tall buildings toward his hotel. All four of the men slowly began to follow him into the darkness, picking up their pace as they got closer. Unaware of their presence and uncertain of his route to his hotel, the businessman's life was about to change—permanently.

WHAT TO DO, WHAT NOT TO DO:

In this example, the out-of-town businessman needs to be aware that he does not know the area well and instead should focus all of his attention on where he is heading. It is likely that local criminals who regularly work the area around the conference center can quickly spot a visiting businessman. In this case, they promptly sized up the businessman as an easy mark and determined he was not a hard target. If the businessman exuded confidence and was more aware of his surroundings, moving deliberately and **limiting his exposure to where the criminals could get to him** to commit the crime, he would have been in a much better situation.

The businessman needs to remember to **"keep his head on a swivel"** to at least allow the possibility of detecting the group of criminals. Even if he did not immediately see them, he would have at least had a fighting chance or may have sensed that something was wrong prior to getting attacked. Most importantly, put the phone away. **Text or call when you are safely at your destination**, not while out on the street in the middle of an unfamiliar city and fully exposed as a target.

The smarter move would have been to **take a taxi or a commercial transportation provider** directly to the hotel. Transportation is readily available outside the conference center lobby, especially at the end of the day. Another good choice would have been to stick together with other conference attendees, traveling to the hotel and enjoying dinner as a group. You do not want to get separated from the crowd and go off on your own at an out-of-town conference if you can avoid it.

RUNNING ERRANDS

Running errands is a part of life for almost everyone. You may have a weekly routine, perhaps after work on certain days or on weekends, where you and your loved ones go to purchase goods and services or tend to your family's needs. Your errands might include purchasing food at the grocery store or a membership wholesale club, a big-box retail store, a home improvement warehouse, or smaller establishments such as a local dry cleaner or a mom-and-pop store. In this section, some security comments and strategies will be offered to keep in mind for specific locations.

LOOK TWICE TIP

The Best Time to Run Errands

Run your errands at odd times when most people are off doing something else, perhaps earlier in the morning when stores first open or at night just before they close. The roads will tend to have fewer cars and less traffic congestion, making your trip quicker. Your unusual timing may reward you with less foot traffic in and around the stores. Fewer vehicles and a reduced amount of foot traffic may result in a less stressful experience overall, and **you will have an easier time maintaining awareness of who is around you on the roads and inside the stores.**

If the option presents itself, running errands when stores first open in the morning is likely the best plan. Some of the potential adversaries you might normally encounter on the street are likely still asleep after a long night of intoxicated debauchery or harassing other good citizens like you and your loved ones. Get your errands done before these adversaries even wake up. **AVOID, AVOID, AVOID.**

1) Twenty-four-hour convenience stores and gas stations.

Depending on the area, be wary of these locations, especially at night. There is a reason you often see security precautions in place for the employee who is taking care of the store and the associated gas station. A few of these precautions may include security cameras, protective barriers around the cash register, and **height strips** by the entry/exit doors to help gauge the height of robbers rushing out of the store. Local convenience stores have a reputation for high cash turnover, are frequently open all night with only one employee on duty, sell alcohol and cigarettes in many states, and are a welcoming sight in most neighborhoods. A range of people often want to loiter in the parking lot in their cars or sit along the front of the store, waiting for something interesting to happen. **When possible, this is a location best visited during the daytime, especially when there is a large amount of vehicle and foot traffic in the store and outside by the gas pumps.** Be aware of your surroundings and who is in close proximity to you in the parking lot, the store, and while pumping gas.

Some gas stations in tough neighborhoods have gone so far as to post stickers on the gas pumps that say, "Look Around! Pay attention while pumping gas!" **A wise person once called this a CLUE**—this area has had problems before and likely will again. When filling your vehicle with gasoline, you are exposed as a target. You may be focused on pumping gas, cleaning car windows, or checking your vehicle's oil level; you may be mesmerized by the television screen that starts playing videos and advertisements once the gas starts pumping. All of these distractions provide a great opportunity for a quick "smash and grab" robbery—possibly by armed criminals—while there is little chance for you to successfully escape in your vehicle. Security cameras will just serve to record the identity-concealing clothing choices and fancy footwork of the criminals as they escape into the local community, never to be caught.

So, what should you do? Avoid going during the night; frequent the gas station when other customers are present. Be extremely vigilant and observant. Appear confident, not paranoid or jumpy. Pump your gas and pay at the pump with a credit card if possible. Closely observe who is loitering nearby or if someone starts moving in your direction on foot. If you have a second person with you in the vehicle, you can "set up security" by having the other person provide a continuous 360-degree lookout in a natural, non-alerting manner. This second person can quietly provide verbal updates about what is happening around the periphery of your vehicle to avoid surprises and allow time to react if necessary. **ALWAYS KEEP YOUR CAR KEY OR KEY FOB ON YOUR PERSON WHILE AT A GAS STATION. NEVER LEAVE YOUR KEYS IN YOUR CAR WHILE PUMPING GAS, EVEN FOR A FEW BRIEF MOMENTS. LADIES, DO NOT LEAVE YOUR KEY OR KEY FOB IN YOUR HANDBAG INSIDE YOUR VEHICLE WHILE PUMPING GAS.**

If attacked, you and others in your vehicle should attempt to **GET OFF THE X** and run away to a safe location, call for help, and come back for your vehicle once the criminals depart. Once well away from your vehicle and in a safe spot, lock your car via your key fob remote if still within range and if it is safe to attempt. Without your car key or key fob, most criminals attempting to carjack your vehicle will have a very difficult time and will likely depart the crime scene empty-handed just as quickly as they appeared. **Your vehicle and its contents are not worth dying over.**

WHAT TO DO, WHAT NOT TO DO

Gone in a Flash

The following example demonstrates why you should never leave your keys inside your vehicle or your ignition at the gas station. In one recent daytime situation in the Northeastern United States, a person left their keys in their car after filling up with fuel. They stepped away into the gas station convenience store for just a moment. In seven seconds (yes, SEVEN seconds), a team of observant criminals pulled up in a car. One member of the criminal team jumped out of the vehicle and entered the victim's car, and both cars drove off at high speed. The victim had their car stolen in exactly seven seconds during the day, fully documented on security camera footage at the gas station convenience store. This was easily avoidable if the victim had just taken their keys into the convenience store and locked their car. The criminals must have been located nearby, waiting for exactly this type of opportunity, and seeing an opening, they acted briskly.

The moral of the story: If you make the mistake of leaving your keys in your car and you encounter a prepared adversary, expect that the criminals will depart in your vehicle, and you will have to find alternate transportation to get home. Do not leave your keys in your vehicle when you step away, even for a few brief moments.

2) Big-box stores.

Big-box stores include large department stores, membership wholesale clubs, and home improvement warehouses, among others. Common security features include a substantial number of security cameras monitored by a professional security staff. Some stores may employ an armed off-duty police officer in uniform to provide a ready response and arrest authority as required; others may have a uniformed security guard with a radio who is trained to call police if needed. The time delay between an initial call for help and the police arriving to respond to a situation in progress in these large stores has been a challenge, with some of the larger incidents and their dramatic impact reported in national news. It is prudent to take the time to identify the locations of emergency exits in the stores where you regularly shop. Learn how to get to the rear exit of the store in case you have to depart quickly in an emergency. Also, identify the locations of any emergency exits on the sides of the building if present.

3) Smaller stores (such as a dry cleaner or mom-and-pop shop).

Smaller stores often have little to no budget for security. These establishments potentially have security cameras observing the front and rear doors and maybe one camera overlooking the cash register. Some of these cameras could just be for show to scare off criminals and may not function properly or do not record the video feed. In other cases, the cameras are fully operational and continuously record the video feed to an off-site server, where it is stored for a lengthy period of time. Many smaller stores will have two entrances/exits: one in the front and one in the back for deliveries. Just be aware that in smaller stores, you will likely have to take care of yourself without assistance in case of a security incident.

4) Grocery stores.

Grocery stores can be large or small, but they tend to have certain features in common. Most midsize to large grocery stores have an entrance/exit at the front of the store, with large glass windows allowing observation into and from the parking lot. Emergency exits are located on the sides of the store, and delivery access is at the rear of the store. This can serve as an emergency egress route if necessary. Other than some security cameras throughout the store and in the cash register area, there will be little to no other security preparations. Be aware of the locations of emergency exits in your regular store in case you have to exit quickly.

5) Open-air markets (such as a farmer's market).

These markets generally have no security measures in place. Based on the open-air design, patrons can approach the market from almost limitless directions on foot without any entry requirements or challenges. There is no security camera coverage; if paying in cash, the identity of patrons remains unknown. Many of these markets have no law enforcement or security presence. Due to very limited hours of operation (perhaps five or six hours on a Saturday morning), there tends to be a high density of people in the market at any given time. Although most of the patrons are friendly, nice people just looking for great food or bargains, be aware of who is around you while shopping in these markets. Criminals may be drawn to these events, which serve as an excellent location for pick-pocketing and purse snatching. An unlocked car parked nearby would be easy to rummage through without drawing much attention due to the large turnover of people, many of whom do not know each other, nor do they know who is associated with which car. Of concern, this type of environment may have the potential for a mass shooting with little to no immediate security response to decisively end an attack.

6) Fast food restaurants and drive-through lanes.

Fast food restaurants are a common sight throughout most cities in the United States. Many have a drive-through lane associated with the restaurant. Although usually safe, it is important to evaluate the security concerns associated with a drive-through lane. Some drive-throughs have a concrete barrier that separates the drive-through lane from the rest of the parking lot surrounding the supported restaurant. While waiting in line in your car, your movement is extremely limited, and you are essentially trapped in the lane. This is especially true if you have other waiting vehicles idling in front of and behind your vehicle. If an adversary approaches your vehicle on foot while you are trapped in line, you cannot readily pull forward or back up. **Your best chance to defend against an adversary on foot may be to exit your vehicle on the opposite side and run away, but only if you identify the threat approaching and still have enough time to break contact.** The only other option is to ensure your car windows are closed, and all vehicle locks are fully engaged to keep an attacker at bay, but this is very limited protection against a motivated adversary who seeks to commit an armed robbery or cause physical harm. You are a sitting duck in your stationary vehicle, essentially at the criminal's mercy. If there is no vehicle to your immediate front or rear, seek to drive your car forward or backward in an attempt to **GET OFF THE X** and escape.

Instead of waiting in a drive-through lane, consider parking your vehicle in a safe location and enter the restaurant on foot. This offers a greater opportunity to observe what is happening in the immediate vicinity of the parking lot and the restaurant and enables you to take action as necessary. Keep your options open. If there are security concerns related to walking from the parking lot to the restaurant, it is time to change your plans and eat at another location in a different area of the city.

Maintain Proper Vehicle Distance

All too often, when in slow-moving or standstill traffic, drivers pull up right behind the car to their immediate front, which eliminates their ability to steer out of a problem. **When in slow-moving or nearly stationary traffic, you should try to keep at least one car length of space between your vehicle bumper and the vehicle in front of you to maintain the ability to steer your vehicle out of a problem.** This is not always possible in a city environment because other drivers may try to aggressively cut in front of your vehicle and fill the empty space. Do your best.

7) Shopping mall complex.

Shopping malls offer a large number of stores in a welcoming environment and have been a favorite of Americans for many years. Most malls have security protocols in place, including closely monitored security cameras, patrolling security guards, frequent visits by uniformed armed law enforcement officers, and private plainclothes security personnel working within some of the larger stores in the complex. Duress buttons with visible lights and audible alarms are installed in some less-traveled mall corridors or in parking garages or parking lots. Be aware of low-level criminal activity around the exterior of the shopping mall, especially after dark. Depending on the area, some malls have experienced car break-ins, robberies, and purse snatchings. There has been an increase in gang activity in and around many mall complexes, including fights between rival gangs. A few shopping malls have even been targeted by mass shooters over the past several years with horrific results.

What should you do? There are several steps to take. First, be careful when selecting a parking spot. Parking is always at a premium around malls, and the best spots quickly fill up during business hours. At a minimum, ensure that you remember exactly where you parked to avoid spending a lot of time searching for your vehicle after you leave the interior of the mall complex. It is difficult to defend yourself and your loved ones while distracted searching for your vehicle, especially if your hands are filled with multiple shopping bags containing all of your purchases. Criminals will view a distracted shopper loaded down with several bags as a prime target for a quick "smash and grab" robbery.

Prior to entering the mall, use your mobile phone to take a photo that shows where your vehicle is parked, including the exact level in the parking garage and any associated parking spot number. This photo can also serve as documentation if your vehicle is stolen from the shopping facility. **If you are the victim of a robbery, remember that "things" can be replaced. Your life and the lives of your loved ones are precious and are all that matter. If a robber wants your stuff, give it to him so that you can live another day.**

Second, know the basic floorplan of your local shopping mall. Learn where the exits are located and how to depart the building quickly in case of an emergency. You want to know exactly how to get outside as quickly as possible so that you can run away to safety. Stay up to date on local news and know if your shopping mall faces challenges from gang activity. Consider shopping at the mall as soon as it opens, prior to some of the local youths or gang members arriving to hang out and look for trouble. These young people are more likely to visit the mall after school in the middle of the afternoon, in the evenings, or on weekends.

In case of violence in a shopping mall, **GET OFF THE X**

immediately and move to a position of safety where you are shielded from observation and protected from the effects of gunfire. Seek to get outside of the mall as quickly as possible, and do not stop until you are a safe distance away. Once in a safe location, call for help and remain on the phone. Stay close to the ground, making yourself a smaller target. **Do not waste time trying to get to your car and drive away from the mall. Even if you reach your vehicle, you will have to deal with a flood of other cars trying to get out of the parking lot, resulting in a traffic jam. This is not an effective strategy. Instead, move on foot.** Once the situation is fully resolved, you can return for your vehicle. In the meantime, ensure you and your loved ones physically depart the proximity of the mall complex to provide for your continued safety.

LOOK TWICE TIP

The Perils of Stairwells

Stairwells are often a magnet for crime. Depending on the building, many stairwells lack security cameras and have limited foot traffic. Once you enter a stairwell, you are more isolated, with limited options to quickly escape.

Criminal activities in stairwells have historically included illicit drug sales and use, as well as assaults. In some cities, muggers wait in **stairwells of parking garages** for the occasional impatient person who chooses to take the stairs when the elevator is too slow or out of service, especially at night.

When you have a choice, it is better to take an elevator to go between floors in a parking garage, a business building, or even a large condominium or apartment building. When taking the elevator, you are more likely to be around other people and have security camera coverage monitored by professional security guards. The lighting in the vicinity of an elevator bank tends to be an improvement over a dimly lit stairwell. You are less restricted in your movements prior to entering the elevator; in a stairwell, you can only go up or down, and you might be locked out from reentering the interior of the building on certain floors. If you find yourself in a physical altercation, there is a significant risk of falling or getting pushed down the stairs. **When you have a choice, avoid stairwells.**

One exception to consider is a mass shooting in a shopping mall complex. If you need to exit a shopping mall rapidly, it may be prudent to enter into a stairwell, quickly change levels, and then escape to the outside of the building. In this specific circumstance, the stairwell may offer temporary visual **CONCEALMENT** from a shooter's observation for you and your loved ones. It is much harder for a shooter to engage a target that they cannot see. The stairwell may also provide protection from the effects of gunfire (**COVER**) due to the construction of the walls and by rapidly changing from one floor to another (altitude change), which keeps you out of the direct line of fire. Aggressively **KEEP MOVING** until you have exited the building and reached a position of safety well away from the mall.

MEDICAL FACILITIES AND PHARMACIES

1) Hospitals.

Hospitals are generally a safe place and can be viewed as a **HARD POINT** as you are moving around town. Almost every hospital has a substantial security presence of some type, and many facilities have professional armed security guards. Security cameras and other security protocols have been installed throughout the various buildings and common areas that comprise a hospital complex. Police officers and other First Responders are also frequently seen in and around hospitals, increasing their level of security.

2) Pharmacies.

Pharmacies can be viewed as regular stores from a security standpoint, but be wary when returning to your vehicle. Some criminals may be interested in stealing your prescription medicines for resale on the black market, and they will not know what prescriptions you have until after they steal your shopping bag. Pay close attention to anyone who is lingering near the exit of the store, both inside and outside. Also, observe individuals loitering in peripheral areas of the parking lot and paying close attention to customers exiting the store. These people may be assessing whether or not you are a good target. Some criminals work in teams, and a person in the store may assess you as a soft target and then text or call their teammate outside to be ready for your exit. If you have concerns, ask the store manager to have an employee walk you to your vehicle and remain nearby until you depart.

3) Community health centers.

These facilities are also known as medical clinics in some areas and offer services more closely related to those of an urgent care facility than a hospital. Expect a reduced security presence, if any, due to tighter budgets than many hospitals. Apply the same protocols that you would use when exiting a pharmacy, staying aware and observing any individuals who are loitering around the exit or in the parking lot. Some criminals would welcome the opportunity to steal medications from patients exiting a community health center. Do not make their task easy.

Know Where the Hard Points Are Located

Plan ahead and learn where potential **HARD POINTS** are located in your neighborhood, especially in areas that you or your loved ones frequent. In case of trouble, you will know immediately where to go to find a safe haven and get help.

SCHOOL

School security is of the greatest importance to most towns across the country. Experts from all levels of active law enforcement and certain private security specialists are focused full-time on developing policies, procedures, and techniques to deal with the issue of school violence in all its forms. **You are encouraged to contact your local school officials and law enforcement agencies directly to gain a complete understanding of the specific policies and guidance related to school security that are already in place in your local schools.** This way, the entire community and school system can employ the same tailored, expert guidance to confront school security issues in all forms without offering potentially conflicting guidance.

HANGING OUT WITH FRIENDS

Choose your friends carefully, especially when moving to a new city and starting a fresh chapter in your life. Any new friend is a relatively unknown person to you. Until you have spent a significant amount of time with your new friend across a wide range of situations, you will not have a full appreciation for the breadth of their character, including their habits, preferences, and personal history.

If you choose poorly when selecting a new friend, you may find yourself suddenly thrust into disturbing or illegal situations that can catch you off guard. Your new friend may introduce some close contacts who make you uneasy and with whom you do not want to associate. Your new friend may reveal their personal involvement in the use of illegal drugs or other illicit activities without warning, putting you in a difficult position, and you could find yourself caught up in a situation that quickly spirals out of your control. This is especially true when moving from a small town in middle America to a big city. Remain vigilant and use caution when initially visiting a new friend in their residence or going out on the town together because their lifestyle choices may directly impact you if you get caught up in their scene.

AT THE BANK OR ATM

Banks go to great lengths to protect their customers and create a safe experience. The inside of a bank branch building can generally be regarded as a **HARD POINT** if you are out in the community and need to seek safety during business hours. Once you depart the bank building and head back out into the local neighborhood, you promptly leave the protective security umbrella provided by the bank. Criminals may choose to target you when you depart the bank, hoping to steal any cash that you withdrew while inside. This is even more likely if the criminal observes you making a withdrawal from an **Automated Teller Machine (ATM)** in the bank's vestibule or in the immediate vicinity of the bank building.

If you need to make a withdrawal from an ATM, it is best to use a machine located inside the main lobby of a bank building. The second-best choice is to use an ATM built into the wall in a bank's vestibule, just inside the outer doors. The third-best choice is to use an ATM that is built into the outside wall structure of a bank building, but be aware of who is around you and note if you may be under observation by someone loitering in the area.

Avoid using stand-alone ATMs that are located in convenient locations around a city, separate from a bank, regardless of the time of day. These ATMs can often be found in small neighborhood convenience stores. In one major Northeastern city, dozens of these stand-alone ATMs were violently ripped out of multiple convenience stores and stolen in brazen attacks over just a six-month period. It is best to avoid using these freestanding machines.

Depending on the neighborhood, pay close attention while sitting in your vehicle in the drive-through lane at a bank for either teller services or while using a drive-up ATM. Although the area is almost always covered by security cameras, a criminal could walk up to your car at the completion of the transaction and rob you of whatever cash you just received and then run away, unlikely to be caught. This comes down to the **POSSIBLE VERSUS THE PROBABLE**. Although possible, is this a **PROBABLE** event at your local bank? You will have to judge for yourself based on available crime data and what you learn about the neighborhood. You may be mostly safe; if not, make appropriate choices to mitigate the risk.

What are some other options? How can you mitigate the risks of using an ATM or going to a bank building? Below are a few choices to consider.

1) Go digital and avoid using cash when possible.

Use a debit card or credit card instead of cash for all purchases. If you are uncomfortable with a credit card due to the associated high-interest charges and fees, choose to use the card as a "charge card." Only purchase items within your budget and then pay off the credit card balance in full every month. With this method, you have the protection and convenience of using a credit card without facing any additional interest charges. You will not need to carry much cash, and visits to the ATM will be infrequent.

2) Conduct all of your banking online through the bank's mobile app or internet website.

By using a mobile device (anywhere) or a computer in the safety and comfort of your home, you physically separate yourself from a bank building. This **LIMITS YOUR EXPOSURE** and mitigates risk.

3) Go with friends.

If you must use an ATM, go during the daytime and bring a couple of friends along. "Safety in numbers" is a simple but often true mantra and may cause a criminal to choose a softer target to pursue. Security does not have to be hard or tricky; oftentimes, it just stems from considering alternatives and making smart choices.

Another option is to visit the ATM with a friend or two and have another friend pull up nearby in a vehicle at the end of your transaction so you can jump into the waiting car and promptly depart the area. This technique will quickly put distance between you and the ATM, thwarting any would-be attacker.

Using a Throw-Away Wallet

When confronted by a robber who demands your money, one technique is to **visibly pull out your wallet, throw it on the ground in one direction, and run in the other direction**. The robber will tend to move toward the wallet (and money), offering a potential chance to escape and **GET OFF THE X**. Whether to apply this technique or another variation is a judgment call, but it provides you with an option.

A variation of this technique involves using a **throw-away wallet**. Keep a small amount of money in a cheap, traditional-style wallet, perhaps in your back pocket. Carry a money clip or minimalist-style wallet in your front pocket with the rest of your cash, credit cards, driver's license, etc. If confronted by a robber, pull out your traditional wallet from your back pocket and throw it in one direction. Run in the other direction. This way, the criminal only gets a cheap wallet with a few dollars instead of all your cash, credit cards, or other credentials.

Remember that **no amount of money is worth your life.** Use your best judgment on what action to take. **Observe key details about the overall robbery and specifics about the robber** to report later to law enforcement after you survive the attack.

COMMUNITY CENTERS

Community centers offer a broad spectrum of activities and sports that appeal to all ages and can be a great place to meet people and spend leisure time. Some community centers also focus on providing young people with competitive sports activities after school or in the evenings to keep them off the streets. The management team will likely incorporate basic security planning into the day-to-day operations of their facility since maintaining a safe environment for all patrons is an essential part of their charter.

Pay close attention to the vicinity outside of your community center as you develop a **BASELINE** for the neighborhood. Many centers are safe and filled with positive energy. People are naturally drawn to this type of social environment. Unfortunately, some wayward members of the neighborhood may also be drawn to the excitement around the community center, but for different reasons. Instead of participating in this positive setting, they bring their obnoxious social skills and illicit activities to the environment. These individuals are not welcome by the management team or other patrons, so they tend to stay outside and look for trouble. If you see these bad apples, remain vigilant and **AVOID** contact.

PARKS AND EXERCISE PATHS

Parks and exercise paths are great for pursuing your physical fitness goals, whether playing sports, running, or walking. They are also good locations to relax and enjoy the outdoors or for young children to build their dexterity and strength on playground equipment. Keep your security in mind to ensure a safe and positive experience.

1) AVOID PATTERNS in your workouts.

If you like to run or walk, avoid going on the same route at the same time on the same days each week. Change it up a bit; have multiple running routes and alter the time you run, if possible. Switching your exercise time by thirty or forty-five minutes earlier or later may be enough to throw off the timing of a would-be stalker or attacker. Do not be predictable.

2) Know where the HARD POINTS are located along your exercise routes.

If you are running or walking on an exercise path and something bad happens, it is important to have identified well in advance where the nearest HARD POINTS are located along the route where you can quickly go to find safety and call for help. Does your route pass by a police precinct? Is there a hospital close by? Commit to memory all of the possible HARD POINTS along your various exercise routes.

3) Identify vulnerable points on your exercise routes.

No route is perfect. If there are portions of your exercise routes where you are more vulnerable, such as a short section through the woods or a segment along the edge of a tough neighborhood, be aware of these locations. Stay vigilant and be prepared to "turn on the jets" and run away at top speed to **GET OFF THE X**. If possible, either limit or completely eliminate these vulnerable points on your exercise routes. If you receive unwelcome attention on one of your routes, do not use it again for several weeks or dismiss the route altogether.

4) Work out with a fitness partner or join an exercise group.

Exercising with a partner or a workout group makes pursuing your fitness goals even more fun. It can help to maintain motivation and encourage you to stick with your fitness plan even when you want to take the day off. It also improves your everyday security through "safety in numbers." If you are in trouble or injured, your workout partner or a member of the group can call for help or assist you in moving to safety. You are a HARDER TARGET when exercising with a partner or a workout group.

5) Headphones or earbuds.

Take extra care when wearing headphones or earbuds while working out in parks or on exercise paths. It can be enjoyable to have music or other entertainment for motivation or to help pass the time while you are working out. The downside is that headphones or earbuds often limit or even eliminate your ability to hear what is going on around you. This is especially important during a workout on an exercise trail where you are **EXPOSED** to threats and possibly isolated from others. If you cannot hear what is going on in your immediate surroundings or when a potential attacker is approaching, then you are at a significant disadvantage. Limiting your hearing unnecessarily **INCREASES YOUR RISK**.

WHAT TO DO, WHAT NOT TO DO

Gone in a Flash

The family of four headed to the local park to spend some time together throwing a couple of flying discs. Moving to a large open area on the side of the park, the mom and dad each began tossing a disc to their two small children, a five-year-old boy and a six-year-old girl. The discs were flying back and forth, and everyone was enjoying themselves.

After a while, the five-year-old boy seemed to lose interest and started playing with crabapples lying on the ground in the nearby vicinity, following a trail of the fruits back to the tree from which they fell. The parents and the young daughter continued throwing both flying discs back and forth, and with only three players remaining, the game picked up speed.

Just a few moments later, the father looked around and said, "Where is our son?" The family abruptly stopped the game, and the father, mother, and daughter started looking in earnest for the missing boy. The mother said in a panicked voice, "He was here just a moment ago! Where could he have gone?" After several minutes of desperate searching, it was clear that the boy was no longer in the park.

The local police precinct was located not far from the park, and the family rushed over to ask for help. The police immediately took down the necessary information, and two plainclothes detectives and a few uniformed police officers fanned out in the area to start searching for the missing boy. Within minutes, the police dispatcher radioed that a boy had been found and was sitting in the town library a block away down the street. He matched the description of the missing five-year-old.

The family and one of the detectives rushed to the library, where the parents were relieved to see their son sitting with a librarian and another woman, drinking some water. The woman told the family she had found the boy on the edge of the park walking alone and that he had told her he was lost. She had taken him to the nearby library to call the police and report the missing child.

The parents asked their son why he wandered off. He said, "I was looking at the crabapples, and I got confused in the woods and did not know where to go. I walked over to the sidewalk, and this woman spoke with me. I walked with her because she seemed nice."

The detective said that he had seen this happen before.

He said, "Keep a very close eye on your children in the park. They can disappear in literally a flash."

This family was fortunate and quickly found their missing son. Some other families may not have such a happy ending.

WHAT TO DO, WHAT NOT TO DO:

When in a park, ensure you **keep a constant eye on your children** to avoid a tragedy. Do not let your children out of your sight. In this situation, the family was having a great time but failed to pay close attention when the son started playing on his own with the crabapples and then walked off into the woods. The boy was playing along the edge of the woods for a while, still in plain sight, which caused the parents to let down their guard. Although they did not view this activity as a problem, the child then slipped deeper into the woods and completely disappeared from view. The family should have seen this action and immediately stopped the boy to keep him close by and within their view.

After exiting the woods onto the nearby sidewalk, the young boy said he walked with the woman because she was "nice." Fortunately, the woman turned out to be a good person, and she promptly brought the boy to the local library to contact authorities, reuniting the child with his family. In other cases, the woman could have just as easily turned out not to be so nice, and the outcome would have been very different.

It is likely that this family will not make the same error again. Both parents learned an important lesson in this situation and avoided a tragedy. Learn from their mistakes and protect your loved ones.

LOOK TWICE TIP

CCTV Surveillance Trailers

If you observe a **law enforcement solar CCTV sur-veillance trailer** when you are out in town while running errands, shopping, or in a park, this is a clear sign that local law enforcement officials believe this area requires additional surveillance coverage. Ask yourself, why this particular area? Take note and increase your level of awareness.

Most law enforcement agencies operate on a limited bud-get and do not have an endless supply of these expensive solar trailers. Officials carefully place this equipment in key locations around the community where the additional surveil-lance will have the maximum effect on crime.

If you see a trailer in a shopping center parking lot or a town park, it is **PROBABLE** that the area has experienced increased levels of crime. At a minimum, the police believe it is necessary to have an expanded surveillance capability in the area to serve as a deterrent. This equipment also allows police to observe if a crime occurs so that officers can deploy to stop the crime and make an arrest. If the crime has ended by the time police arrive, the recorded video feed can provide important evidence to support an investigation and prosecution. If you see this type of equipment in your vicinity, stay alert to **MITIGATE RISK**.

RELIGIOUS FACILITIES

Whether a church, synagogue, mosque, or other house of worship, many religious facilities have a robust, detailed security plan in place. Attacks, active shooters, and protesters have struck houses of worship many times in recent memory at locations across the country. Worship leaders have been forced to take steps to address these threats. Many religious leaders have worked in close cooperation with law enforcement and private security consultants to develop full security plans complete with active measures in case of attack. Off-duty uniformed and plainclothes law enforcement officers, along with private armed security guards, are a frequent presence in religious facilities during hours of worship or peak foot traffic. With the increased risk faced by most houses of worship today, many facilities have stepped up to the task and are fully prepared to protect their congregations.

Always be observant and aware while you are in a religious facility, whether for worship, meetings, or any other purpose. Report any concerns promptly to security officials or church leadership so the security plan can be put into action as needed. Be aware of the location of all exits, especially those closest to where you and your loved ones are worshipping in the main sanctuary. Know how to depart the sanctuary quickly when the lights are on and also when the room is darkened. Given the choice, sit close to an emergency exit door so that if active hostilities break out or some type of an incident occurs, you and your loved ones can get out of the main sanctuary within seconds and quickly move through a side corridor. **GET OFF THE X** as quickly as possible and move well away from the incident. Put distance between you and the "X." Exit the building and keep going until you are a significant distance away, fully out of view of any adversary and behind something solid like a building or a thick wall that offers substantial protection from possible gunfire. Call for help and stay on the phone.

Ensure to talk with your family members in advance about what to expect should a situation occur. Be clear about what steps you will take together so that every member of your family knows what to do and where to go. Move as a family; **use CHAINING as a technique to prevent getting separated.** The family leader steps out first and extends one of their arms bent at a ninety-degree angle; the other hand is free to push or open doors, move people or objects out of the way, etc. The next family member links one of their arms through the extended arm ahead of them and then extends their other arm toward the rear at ninety degrees. The next family member links one of their arms through the extended arm ahead of them, and so on, for the rest of the family. This technique allows you and your family or group to hook together with your arms in a strong way that can limit or even eliminate separation when moving together through darkness, smoke, chaotic crowds, or other stresses. Practice this technique as a family so that it becomes second nature.

LARGE EVENTS (SPORTING EVENTS, CONCERTS, PARADES)

Large sporting events and concerts consistently have significant security measures in place to screen for weapons and ensure a safe, positive experience for all attendees. Some issues, however, are difficult to prevent and may still happen regardless of the security measures that are put in place. Sports fans who have attended a hockey match or a football game may have seen a few overly enthusiastic fans square off and get into a fistfight during the event after consuming a few beers. Fights like this may be difficult to prevent a hundred percent of the time, but the event security staff will promptly address the issue and remove the involved parties from the facility. If you are near some fans who start a physical altercation, get out of the way. Do not attempt to intervene in someone else's fistfight; remember to **AVOID** trouble. Your involvement will generally not prove helpful, and you are just asking for trouble to come into your life.

Of greater concern is the targeting of young women and girls at these events, as detailed in the following scenario.

WHAT TO DO, WHAT NOT TO DO

The Invisible Network

Clarissa was excited. She had just turned sixteen years old a few days earlier, and her big birthday present was going to see her favorite professional sports team play one of their biggest rivals at the sports center downtown.

Finally, the big day arrived, and she headed to the sports center with her parents and two younger brothers. The seats were ideal and offered a great close-up view of the game. The competition between the two teams was intense, and the roar of the crowd heightened the thrill of the experience. Her father bought food for the family, and she was enjoying eating a hot dog and drinking a cold soda with her brothers. Everything was perfect. Clarissa told her mother she urgently needed to use the restroom after drinking so much soda. Her mom told her to go to the restroom just outside their section and hurry back afterward. Clarissa headed off to the restroom, her petite figure moving alone up the stairs and out of view.

The family continued to watch the game, cheering as the teams wrestled for control of the match. The mood was electric, and the roar of the crowd was deafening. Lost in the moment, no one in Clarissa's family noticed the time passing by so quickly. Suddenly, Clarissa's mom looked around and noticed her daughter had not returned from the restroom. She seemed startled and immediately grew concerned. Pulling out her phone, she texted Clarissa. No reply. She then tried to call but could not hear well due to the noise of the crowd; there was no answer. She tugged on her husband's arm and said, "I am going to look for Clarissa. She should have been back by now." The mom briskly headed out toward the restroom.

After making her way up the stairs, the mother arrived at the restroom and entered. Looking around, she saw no sign of Clarissa. Starting to panic, the mom started calling Clarissa's name. She asked a few other women in the restroom if they had seen her daughter and offered a brief description, but they all said no. The mom rushed back to her husband. Now panicked, the family left their seats and moved together until they found a security officer in the outer walkway and told them their daughter was missing. The security officer immediately sent out an alert over the radio, including a description of the young sixteen-year-old girl.

It was too late. Clarissa was already long gone from the sports center and heading out of the city. Drugged and in the back of a van, she had been taken out of the sports center by a woman posing as her mother, who told the security guards that "her daughter" was feeling sick due to a medical condition and she needed to go home and rest. No one challenged the story.

Clarissa was found weeks later in another city a few states away, drugged and working as a prostitute. She had been spotted and grabbed by a human trafficking network that worked at major public events, including the sports facility where Clarissa was taken. The network paid numerous women to drug young victims who were separated from family or friends and promptly removed them from the sports event or concert to a nearby waiting vehicle outside the venue.

WHAT TO DO, WHAT NOT TO DO:

Although large events are generally safe and enjoyable activities, not all participants have good intentions. Keep an extremely close eye on your children, and do not allow them to venture away from other family members without a chaperone. Young women should attend these events with family or friends and stay together at all times. **Constant vigilance will lead to a fun and successful event.**

Parades are an American tradition and have been widely regarded as a safe and fun way to celebrate a particular holiday or event. Unfortunately, most large public gatherings, including parades, now require security planning. Event planners used to just worry about traffic and crowd control along the parade route. As seen in current events, a parade may now be a location that attracts troubled individuals or groups who seek to harm others through a mass attack. The attack may be designed simply to harm as many people as possible, or it may be used to make a political point based on the motivations of the attacker or group.

Prior to attending, ask yourself whether an attack is a **POSSIBLE** or a **PROBABLE** outcome at a specific parade due to the event that is being celebrated. That may be a tough judgment call to make. If you deem the threat to be too high, simply **AVOID, AVOID, AVOID,** and do not attend the parade. If the event is scheduled for broadcast on television, stay at home and watch it from the comfort of your couch. It is important to remember not to live in constant fear. If you want to go to the event, weigh out the risks, and then choose wisely.

If you decide to attend a parade or another large, outdoor public event with open access, use care in choosing the location where you will view the festivities. Attacks could come in many forms. During the Boston Marathon bombing in 2013, two terrorists used homemade pressure cooker bombs to wreak havoc, killing three and wounding hundreds. In Wisconsin in 2021, a man drove an SUV through an annual Christmas parade, killing six and wounding dozens more. At a Fourth of July parade in Illinois in 2022, a suspect was arrested and confessed to killing seven people and wounding dozens more in a mass shooting with a rifle. In any large, outdoor public event with open access, **if you can be seen by an attacker, you are exposed and can be directly engaged.** This is especially true if the attacker takes up a position that affords excellent observation and overwatch along the parade route and chooses to engage with a rifle, particularly one outfitted with a longer barrel and high-end magnified riflescope, allowing for increased accuracy over greater distances.

When considering where to sit or stand when viewing an outdoor public event with open access, understand that attackers often want to make a symbolic statement through their attack. They may be less inclined to attack at the very beginning or end of a parade route, where their horrific efforts may not be as visible to the public. Instead, attacks may be focused closer to the grandstand seating, where the most dazzling parade activities will occur, often with significant media coverage. In the case of a marathon or other long-distance race, the finish line is the most exciting location and a centerpiece of the day's activities. If you wish to mitigate risk, avoid viewing the festivities from these areas.

When possible, stand or sit in front of a hard surface, such as a building or thick wall, so that no one can get behind you. Depending on the construction, this surface may also provide protection to your rear from the effects of gunfire. Concentrate your field of view over the 180 degrees you see from left to right and in front of you. You can effectively discount any issues behind you. This positioning limits your exposure and allows you to pay more attention to the event that you came to enjoy on your immediate front. Keep in mind that even though your back is protected, you are still subject to targeting from an individual with a rifle operating from a high vantage point such as a rooftop or a high-story window. Unless you are hidden from view or inside a building, it is unlikely that you will be able to fully mitigate this risk.

If you are sitting alongside a clump of bushes or a thin material such as plywood or a canvas tent, you are only behind **CONCEALMENT. Concealment protects you from observation. COVER**, on the other hand, **protects you from the effects of weapons such as firearms**. How effective is your choice of COVER? That depends on the power and capability of the weapon that an active shooter is using to shoot at you or the bomb that is detonated in your vicinity.

By standing or sitting with your back to a hard surface such as a wall, you are much less likely to be successfully targeted by a rogue driver who wants to plow through the crowd. A driver, such as the SUV driver in Wisconsin mentioned earlier in this section, likely desires to produce the maximum number of casualties possible. Back up on the sidewalk, against a hard object away from the street, puts you well out of the primary path that this type of attacker will likely take as they aim their vehicle through the crowd.

Another consideration is your **escape route**. If a situation or attack occurs and you and your loved ones need to quickly depart from the area, how do you immediately **GET OFF THE X**? Can you rapidly depart from the main road and duck into an alley or a side street? Is there a building you can slip into? Think ahead as to where you will go. **PLAN AHEAD OR YOU ARE PLANNING TO FAIL**. Consider the size of the crowd, and where you estimate most people will try to run. Will you still be able to execute your plan even if a large number of other people at the event are also trying to escape the vicinity of the attack?

In many instances, the only difference between a routine day and a tragedy is a few seconds and a loud BOOM. The moments immediately preceding an attack often do not offer any noticeable warning signs or clues until an explosion, gunfire, or a chorus of yelling shatters the normalcy of the day.

NIGHT ON THE TOWN

After studying or working hard all week, you may want to reward yourself with some well-deserved relaxation and entertainment. You may enjoy socializing with family and friends, or you just prefer to head out for a night on the town. The security implications of several different types of nightlife are reviewed below.

1) Movie theaters.

When you arrive at a movie theater, identify where each of the emergency exits is located. Consider sitting close to one of these exits in case a situation develops in the theater; you and your loved ones may have an urgent need to instantly depart and **GET OFF THE X**. As you are likely aware, in 2012, an attacker conducted a mass shooting in a theater in Aurora, Colorado with twelve killed and seventy injured. For most communities, such an event is **POSSIBLE but not PROBABLE**. Countless people enjoy movies in theaters across the country every day without any issues. Considering history, however, if you wish to mitigate the risk more fully, you may want to consider investing in a large-screen television and high-end surround sound system. This one-time investment will allow you and your loved ones to watch movies with the latest technology in the safety and comfort of your home. **REDUCE YOUR EXPOSURE** in order to **MITIGATE RISK**.

If you choose to watch a movie in the theater instead of at home, consider sitting further back in the audience for a separate reason. Occasionally, some unruly teenagers purchase hard candy at the concession stand and, during the middle of the movie, hurl the hard candy with great force into the back of the heads of other patrons sitting in the front rows of the theater. At one movie theater in an East Coast city, this happened numerous times during a feature film. It caused such an outcry from those who were struck that the theater management paused the movie in the middle of the film, turned on the overhead lights, and verbally addressed the audience before resuming the film. The perpetrators were never identified. Although not a true security issue, this type of situation is nevertheless frustrating and painful if you are the person who is hit in the head with the hard candy. It makes the movie experience much less fun for you and your loved ones in the theater.

Considering the above issues, some theater management companies provide their staff with night vision devices to scan the audience in the darkness occasionally for potential security threats and identify any obnoxious behavior by young hooligans lacking in manners.

2) Restaurants.

When you dine out in a restaurant, carefully choose your seating location to increase your security. In some restaurants, your choice of table or where you sit may be limited, especially during peak business hours. When possible, sit where you are facing the main entrance door so that you can monitor who enters or exits the establishment. Avoid sitting with your back toward the door, or else you will **INCREASE YOUR RISK** and be surprised by an adversary entering the restaurant and approaching without warning.

Avoid sitting in front of large windows on the front of a restaurant facing the street or a courtyard. If you sit in front of the windows, you visually **EXPOSE** both you and your dining companions to people passing by on the street or even driving by in vehicles. Passersby can easily observe you without your knowledge or awareness. This disadvantage is increased during hours of darkness when you have little to no ability to observe adversaries in the street due to the lights in the restaurant and the darkness outside.

When possible, choose a seating location deeper in the restaurant which is not visible from outside. A booth is usually better than an open table due to increased visual and auditory privacy. Maintain an awareness of who is sitting in other nearby booths when possible.

If you do not have a choice and the restaurant staff sits you and your party at a table, pay close attention to who is sitting at other tables in your vicinity. Floor space comes at a very high premium in the city, and many restaurants maximize profits by increasing the density of tables on the floor to the greatest extent possible. If you are not used to big-city dining, you may find that small tables for a couple can be eighteen inches apart in some restaurants. This results in a complete lack of privacy for your conversations. After living in the city for a while, many people accept this as a routine occurrence, and during their meal, they just ignore other patrons at nearby tables.

Be cautious with this approach, as not all of the other patrons around you may choose to block out your conversations. You do not know who is sitting next to you or what their intentions are. The person could be a reporter for a newspaper or an online blog. They could be a grifter or a petty criminal. Your fellow diners may choose to carefully listen to your every word and exploit the information for their gain after leaving the restaurant. Depending on what you do for a living and if you are under any scrutiny, ALL of the surrounding diners could actually be members of law enforcement or a security service. With the ready availability of modern technology and while sitting in close proximity to your table, those dining nearby could record your entire conversation with great clarity on their mobile device, all without your knowledge or consent.

Considering the lack of privacy in many big city restaurants, it may be prudent to limit the topics of your conversation. Save more sensitive conversations for private dining rooms, booths at a minimum, or other locations away from the restaurant setting. Regardless of the sensitivity of your conversation topics, ensure you maintain complete awareness while enjoying your food and the discussion. Do not get so "zoned in" that you lose awareness as to who is coming and going from the restaurant, activities taking place around you, or other conversations nearby that may prove fruitful for YOUR purposes.

Be careful about **SETTING PATTERNS** by going to the same local restaurant every day or the same day each week at the same time. Mix it up. Otherwise, your **PATTERN OF LIFE** becomes apparent, and the restaurant becomes an easy location for an adversary to "pick you up" and gain information or follow you depending on their goals.

Similar to other public places, identify emergency exits as soon as possible. In an actual emergency, you could also depart out the rear of the establishment, where the restaurant receives deliveries.

3) Bars and nightclubs.

Bars and nightclubs have different security concerns and "personalities" due to differing activities or themes in each type of establishment. The personalities of individual bars and nightclubs can vary widely from upscale and well-mannered to downright dangerous, depending on the clientele they attract. Know where you are going and the reputation associated with the location prior to heading out on the town.

When looking at a bar from a security perspective, evaluate if the establishment caters to a specific group. Is the bar a local haunt for people only from a certain neighborhood? Is it a "biker bar" catering solely to motorcycle enthusiasts or motorcycle club members? Are the patrons of the bar territorial? In each of these circumstances, you may find that you are unwelcome unless you meet the unstated criteria for entry. **If you insert yourself into a place where you do not belong, the security situation may become difficult very quickly and result in an undesired outcome.**

In general, maintain heightened awareness in a bar. In some

establishments, you have little to worry about, and most people are there to drink, socialize, and have a good time. In other bars, you may expose yourself to significantly increased risk; know the reputation of the establishment. If a fight breaks out, stay away; consider leaving immediately. Many bars, especially small local ones, may not actively screen for weapons. If the situation degrades, for whatever reason, leave and go somewhere else. Always **SEEK TO MITIGATE RISK.**

WHAT TO DO, WHAT NOT TO DO

On the Cutting Edge

In a major Southeastern US city, a "good Samaritan" was standing in a bar chatting with friends and enjoying himself. Suddenly, a few feet away, a visibly drunk man aggressively attacked a much smaller, weaker man with whom he had been talking just moments earlier. The drunk man slammed his fists into the face and chest of the smaller man again and again; no one stepped in to help. The smaller man cried out as he tried to shield himself from the powerful blows of the intoxicated attacker. He was clearly overpowered and bleeding, likely from a broken nose.

Seeing the lopsided fight and wanting to assist the smaller man, the good Samaritan instinctively intervened, pulling the attacker off of his victim and temporarily stopping the fight. Angered by the unwanted intervention and without warning, the attacker spun around and pulled a knife on the good Samaritan, slashing wildly at his torso. The good Samaritan was caught off-guard but was able to barely avoid getting cut by the sudden slashing with the knife. He rushed out of the bar to safety.

After calming down later at home, the good Samaritan

realized how close he came to receiving a potentially deadly injury. He told his friends, "I didn't even know the two guys who were fighting; I was just trying to help because the smaller guy was getting pummeled. I wish I had never even gotten involved." His friends agreed, with one commenting that he could have been really hurt or even killed.

WHAT TO DO, WHAT NOT TO DO:

As a general rule, do not get involved in other people's fights, even if you are just trying to defuse the situation or help calm things down. This is an easy way to get hurt, sometimes severely, or you might even be killed. It is always a personal decision; if you see an elderly woman being harshly beaten by a street thug, your moral compass may insist that you take action to save her, regardless of what happens to your personal security or health. **All choices have consequences, good or bad. Weigh out your actions, do what you have to do, but always seek to MITIGATE RISK.**

Protect your drink, no matter what you choose to consume. Maintaining positive control over your drink from the moment the bartender hands you the beverage until you are finished consuming it will eliminate the opportunity for someone to put something into your drink. Do not let your attention be distracted away from your drink; keep it directly in front of you at all times, or else order a replacement. This will lessen the chance of someone spiking your drink with one of the common date-rape drugs or another unwanted substance.

Nightclubs have some differences from bars. The focus tends to be weighted toward the entertainment, with dancing and music provided by a live band or a DJ. Many clubs have well-regulated access and screen by age and attire, among other things. Nightclubs often check to ensure patrons do not bring weapons into the club. Protect your drink just as you would in a bar setting. Nightclubs earn their reputation by the type of clientele that frequent the establishment; know this reputation prior to arrival to avoid problems. Many nightclubs are hotspots for illicit drug trafficking and use. Be wary of who you meet and where you go after departing the club to best protect yourself.

Remember what your mom told you: **NOTHING GOOD HAPPENS AFTER MIDNIGHT.** Crime tends to spike in most cities in the early morning hours. If you choose to stay out on the town until the bars and nightclubs close or until the sun comes up, you are an adult and can make your own choices. You also get to live with the results—good or bad. **MITIGATE RISK** when possible and choose to not stay out until the early morning hours.

4) Parties.

If you host a party or attend one held at a friend's home, you may know most, if not all, of the people who attend. This may provide a potentially safer environment than a bar or nightclub. If you attend a large house party or a fraternity party at an unfamiliar university in a distant city, you will often know very few people. Be aware that these settings do not have the security controls that are present in a well-run nightclub, and unforeseen circumstances may arise quickly. When mixed with alcohol, some situations can spiral out of control and take a dangerous turn due to abuse of controlled substances or interpersonal violence. Be wary, and if you become uncomfortable, leave the party. Think through your transportation plan in advance so you know what you will do if you have to depart quickly.

PART 6

TRANSPORTATION

In the United States, we love to drive, and we treasure our vehicles. This is partly due to the vast size of the country, especially west of the Mississippi River. Driving is the most economical way to cover these great distances, and mass transit is not a valid option in many areas. Our vehicles are often an identity statement that shows the world how we see ourselves and how we wish to be perceived. Our cars often state in not-so-subtle terms what we value and hold dear.

In this chapter, you will be exposed to different modes of transportation, including those that are effective for navigating the city and the surrounding suburbs. Some forms of transportation are especially practical and worthy of your consideration inside the city limits due to the density of streets and the overcrowding of vehicles and people. You will also learn how to **MITIGATE RISK** by softening the statement your vehicle makes about you to others.

AUTOMOBILES

1) Maintenance.

There are certain steps that you should take to ensure your car is fully ready for whatever challenges life may hold. The first item is to perform all necessary maintenance. Either do it yourself or take it to a shop or dealer, but ensure that all of the major systems of the car are well-maintained, with no worn-out parts. **Goal: properly prepare your car so that it does not fail at the moment of truth when you need it most. Your car MUST be reliable.** Proper preventative maintenance will allow your vehicle to remain fully functioning and free of breakdowns as much as possible. No one can predict when a part will fail, but by staying on top of regular maintenance, your car will be less likely to break down.

Pay special attention to the tires. The tires are the only contact between your car and the road. If the tire patch where "the rubber meets the road" loses its grip on the road surface, control of your vehicle will be lost, resulting in a slide or skid. Replace your tires in pairs and always ensure that the tire tread meets or exceeds minimum legal standards.

Maintain maximum visibility from within your vehicle. Does your windshield have any major chips or cracks? Have these defects repaired by a professional auto glass shop, or replace the entire windshield if the damage is extensive. This will ensure your ability to see clearly across the entire windshield. Consider regularly applying a specialized windshield glass water repellent that will make it easier to see in rainstorms. Water will literally run off the windows; use this product on the exterior surface of all of your car windows to maximize your ability to see. When filling up your car with gas, clean the windows regularly with a squeegee and glass cleaner. Dirty windows will reduce your ability to see under demanding driving conditions.

Remove hazing from your headlights to allow a clear, well-lit view at night. Over time, headlights tend to build up a haze on the surface, degrading the headlight performance. This is a slow process, and the degradation may not be noticeable all at once.

Ensure all of your vehicle mirrors are fully functioning. Practice using the rearview mirror and both side-view mirrors to build skill in monitoring cars or people around the exterior of your vehicle.

2) Essential items.

Below are a few items that you should always keep in your car.

—**Jumper cables (battery booster cables)**. Keep these in the trunk in case your vehicle battery dies. Even better, invest in a **portable car battery jump starter** to allow you to jump your own battery without any assistance if your car battery ever dies.

—**LED flashlight.** Purchase a high-quality light-emitting diode (LED) flashlight and fresh batteries. Some of the better

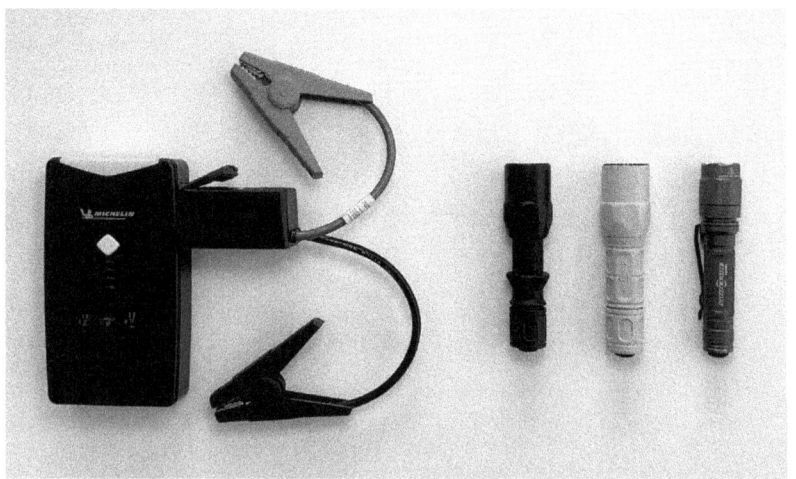

Portable car battery jump starter; various
models of high-quality LED flashlights.

models have a low and high setting. The low setting usually works better inside a car, and the high setting may prove more effective when you are outside of a vehicle. Add a red, green, or blue-green cover or filter on the flashlight to protect night vision. LED flashlights run cooler, last longer, resist breakage, and shine brighter with a much greater number of lumens than a traditional flashlight.

—**Car escape tools**. Tools such as a **window breaker** and a **seat belt cutter** are useful to have close at hand if you or your loved ones need to rapidly escape from a vehicle. A seat belt cutter is a safe way to slice through a heavy-duty seat belt strap. If at all possible, do not use a knife to cut a seat belt in close proximity to the neck or body. Under the stress of an emergency situation, your ability to effectively control a knife may be reduced and could result in a traumatic injury. Combination tools that combine both a window breaker and seat belt cutter are widely available.

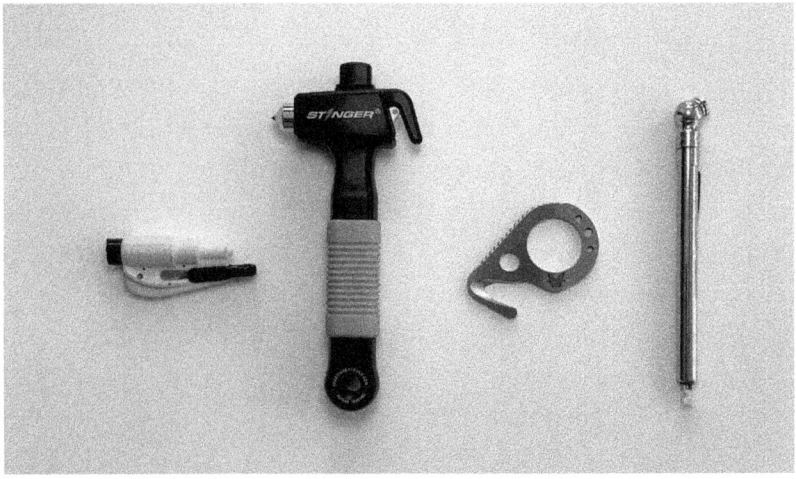

Window breaker and seatbelt cutter (keychain style); window breaker hammer (three-way combination with window hammer, push-style window breaker, and seatbelt cutter); seatbelt cutter tool; pencil-style tire gauge.

—**Tire pressure gauge**. Tire pressure gauges found on air pumps at many service stations are not very accurate, so instead, rely on your own equipment. A high-quality **pencil-style gauge** will accurately measure the actual tire pressure in your vehicle's tires and is quite inexpensive. Another effective option is a **dial-style gauge**. Avoid digital gauges of any style because they contain batteries that must be maintained and could fail at the worst possible time. Due to the extreme temperatures that may be present inside your vehicle in some parts of the country, battery life may be greatly reduced.

—**Global Positioning System (GPS) receiver**. Invest in a portable dedicated GPS receiver designed for use in a vehicle. Some of the more expensive vehicles available today feature a built-in dedicated GPS receiver, but many do not have this feature. A lot of people instead rely on the GPS capabilities of their mobile devices. A mobile device may work most of the time, but if you can afford it, having a dedicated GPS receiver that does not rely on cellular-assisted GPS is preferred. If a large-scale emergency or natural disaster causes the cellular system to overload or break down entirely and temporarily go out of service, or if you are located in a remote area with spotty or no cellular coverage, a dedicated GPS receiver would be money well spent. Make sure to download and apply all software, traffic, and map updates for the GPS receiver at least quarterly to take full advantage of the most current information available.

LOOK TWICE TIP

GPS Receivers

Most dedicated GPS receivers have a "Home" option on the main menu, which, if selected, will guide the GPS receiver

directly to the address that you initially inputted as your residence. If an adversary gains access to your GPS receiver, they
could use this feature to locate where you actually live.

To defeat this issue, **program in an unrelated address
from your local neighborhood as "Home" instead of using
the address of your actual residence**. That way, when you
press "Home" on the GPS, the unit will guide you back to a
location within your local area with which you are familiar,
but your actual residence will not be revealed.

Also, be aware that if an adversary gains access to the
locations and addresses that are programmed into your GPS
receiver or to where you have traveled previously, they will
have significant data to add to their understanding of your
PATTERN OF LIFE. This can potentially be used against you.

—**Entrenching tool (E-tool)**. If you live in an area where your
vehicle might get stuck in either snow or mud, keep an E-tool
in the vehicle. This type of folding shovel is stored easily in the
trunk in a protective carrier and does not take up much space.
If your car or truck gets stuck, an E-tool offers you the ability
to dig out and get your vehicle moving again.

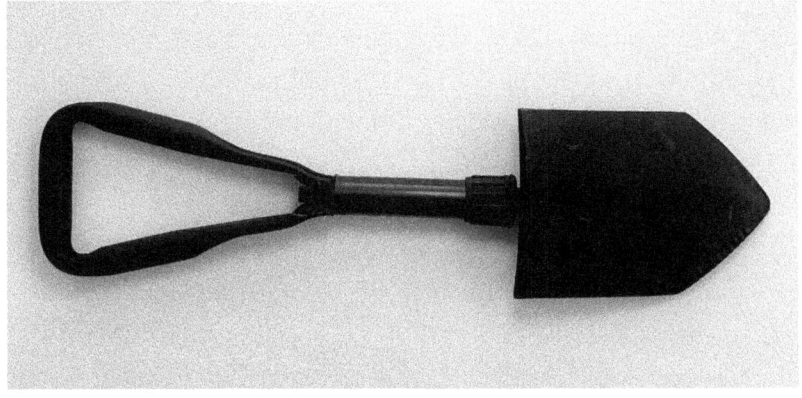

Entrenching tool (e-tool)

—Automobile fire extinguisher. A small auto fire extinguisher is a great piece of emergency equipment that should be standard in every car on the road. This piece of equipment is invaluable if a fire breaks out in your vehicle. Although much more expensive, consider a halon-replacement clean agent fire extinguisher, which is effective for flammable liquids/gases and electrical fires (Class B and Class C). A clean agent extinguisher such as Halotron I extinguishes a fire by displacing oxygen. These agents do not leave a solid residue behind, which can damage your engine or electrical components.

—Locking fuel tank cap. Replace your current standard fuel tank cap with a model that locks with a small key to add another layer of security. **It makes it more difficult for an adversary to put something nefarious into your gas tank.** This is of even greater importance if your vehicle has a gas hatch cover that does not have a privacy locking mechanism and that can be opened by anyone. Either way, a locking fuel tank cap is a smart investment. With the high price of gasoline, adding a locking fuel tank cap also helps to **MITIGATE THE RISK** of having a criminal siphon gas from your vehicle.

—Car safe. A car safe is often referred to as a "car gun safe," "portable security case," "lock box safe," or just a "lockbox." Regardless of terminology, these locking metal containers are constructed of extremely tough metal and are frequently lined with foam or rubber inserts. A security cable that comes with the safe can be wrapped around one of your car seat mounts and then connected to the safe, making it difficult for an adversary to quickly remove the security container from your vehicle. Many models do not have to be permanently mounted. A safe can be concealed easily under a towel or similar covering on the rear floor of most vehicles and carried into a hotel

Car safe/lockbox

for overnight secure storage. This arrangement also allows for access from inside the vehicle. Other mounting options and locations are available depending on the style of safe you choose. These safes are excellent for temporary secure storage of firearms, magazines, ammunition, or valuables such as jewelry or cash.

When considering different locking mechanisms for car safes, a **tube key** is fast and efficient. If the tube key is stored on a car key ring, it will always be available when in the vehicle. Avoid **biometric safes** since they rely on batteries, and the technology is not yet as efficient and fully developed as it may sound. It is important to ensure the ability to access the safe quickly a hundred percent of the time because your life may depend on it. **Combination locks** may be acceptable, but it will be necessary to remember the code and then to physically dial or press the buttons for the combination on the safe under stress, often while your fine motor skills are significantly degraded. Furthermore, if a motivated adversary gains access to your safe for a period of time, they may have the opportunity to run through all of the possible combinations and open the safe.

—**Mobile phone charging cable.** Place a dedicated charging cable in your car for your specific phone model, and never remove it from the vehicle. Most recent car models have one or more Universal Serial Bus (USB) connector ports available. This cable may come in handy to keep your mobile phone fully powered, especially in an emergency.

—**Notebook with pen**. Keep a small spiral notebook with a push-button ballpoint pen within easy reach. Place the notebook on your leg and take notes while driving to record license plate numbers or other details that may quickly slip from memory. The push-button ballpoint pen can be opened and closed with a flick of the thumb instead of having to deal with taking a pen cap on or off or just leaving the ballpoint exposed.

CHECKLIST FOR ITEMS TO KEEP IN YOUR VEHICLE

___ Jumper cables (battery booster cables) or a portable car battery jump starter

___ LED flashlight with batteries

___ Car escape tools (window breaker and seat belt cutter, or a combination tool)

___ Tire pressure gauge

___ GPS receiver

___ Entrenching tool (E-tool)

___ Automobile fire extinguisher

___ Locking fuel tank cap

___ Car safe

___ Mobile phone charging cable

___ Notebook with push button ballpoint pen

3) Exterior preparation.

Observe the outside of any vehicle. What does it say about the occupants? Look at the license plates, bumper stickers, or any words on the car. You can choose to make your car as memorable and unique as you wish, but it may be better to have your vehicle say as little as possible about who is inside. This is part of **LIVING UNDER THE RADAR** or being the **GRAY MAN**. When trying to improve everyday security, one of your primary goals should be to have your vehicle say as little as possible about who is inside. **BLEND IN**. It is your choice.

—**License plates.** Specialty or "vanity" license plates are a visually appealing addition to any vehicle, but they also make a car more memorable to observers. Some plates reflect general interest in or support for a particular cause, organization, or university, while others may have specific requirements that must be proven to order the plate. Special military license plates that show a branch of service or campaign medals, for example, require official United States government proof of service or award documentation of the medal prior to the approval and issuance of the plate. Carefully consider where you live and local attitudes prior to purchasing a specialty plate. Thoughtfully consider if you want to advertise your interests or affiliations to everyone with whom your vehicle comes into contact. In some locations, certain plates may be welcome; in other places, they may generate an angry response based on the affiliation. Think through this prior to mounting a specialty plate on your vehicle.

Some vehicle owners also choose to order personalized license plates that have specific letters or numbers. This makes a license plate extremely memorable to others and would generally be a poor choice from a security perspective. Cars with personalized license plates are easy to follow and can be quickly observed, even in heavy traffic. It is best not to personalize your license plate characters since the plate will be truly one-of-a-kind and may draw too much attention.

Although the number may vary every few years, there are approximately twenty-one states that only require an official license plate to be mounted on the rear of a vehicle. These states have no legal requirement for a front license plate. Residents of these states are free to mount a custom plate on the front of the vehicle if they wish, which shows their interest in a sports team, university, military branch of service, etc. These plates also make your car different and unique and tell others something about your interests. Consider the message that your custom plate sends to others who see it. Is this what you want to say? Or is it just better not to mount a custom plate on the front of your vehicle? Decide what is best for your everyday security.

—**License plate frames.** When sitting at a stop light in traffic, glance at other nearby cars and observe the license plates, especially the rear license plates. It is common to see license plate frames that carry a message. Car dealers often provide a free license plate frame for the rear license plate with the name and location of the dealership or other identifying information when purchasing or leasing a vehicle. This is valuable free advertising for the car dealer.

Since people frequently live in the same town or area as the dealership where they purchased their vehicle, this piece of information can help an adversary narrow down where someone may be from. If your vehicle, for example, has a Texas license plate and an adversary wants to learn more about you and where you reside or spend your time, the plate alone is not much help since Texas is the second-largest state in the United States by size. However, if they see a license plate frame for a car dealer based in Corpus Christi, that is an important detail that can help match other information available about you in databases online. It is unlikely that a person who lives in Dallas or El Paso will travel hundreds of miles to Corpus Christi to purchase a vehicle. This piece of information can help rule out possible identities that reside in distant areas of the state and allow an adversary to focus more closely on data relevant to you.

Some vehicles, possibly including yours, also come with a service plan provided by the dealer, which means the owner will likely return to the dealership for service from time to time. This is a good place for someone to look if they aspire to locate the owner. If an adversary is intent on finding the owner, the dealership has records tying a vehicle to a person's private contact information. $50 paid to an unscrupulous employee at a dealership may yield a home or business address, email address, and likely a phone number ending up in the wrong hands. **It is best to remove any customized license plate frame from your vehicle and replace it with a generic model that offers no information.** Many car dealers also put a sticker or plate on the back of every vehicle they sell or lease with the name of the dealership. The dealer will generally remove this sticker or plate upon your request. Keeping it on the vehicle offers you no advantage.

—**Stickers or emblems.** Have you ever seen a vehicle that is completely covered with bumper stickers on the back? Some cars are adorned with dozens of bumper stickers purchased while visiting tourist attractions across the USA, stickers from universities attended, and every single social or political cause the vehicle owner supports. These stickers offer a lot of personal information about travel history and political leanings that probably should not be shared with every other driver or pedestrian with whom the vehicle comes into contact. If you are one of these people, you may be proud of your broad travels and hold your worldview and political beliefs very strongly, but from a security perspective, it is best to remove all of the stickers and not share this wealth of information. It is a near certainty that someone will be offended by your broad display of stickers, which could result in a random act of violence against you, your loved ones, or your vehicle. Unfortunately, some individuals may choose to "key" your car or slash your tires because they disagree with your expressed views. **LIVE UNDER THE RADAR.**

If you have ever spent time near a military base, you will regularly see car bumper stickers that identify the vehicle owner as a proud member of a particular military branch or perhaps a retiree or veteran. Oftentimes, their entire resume is displayed in colorful stickers on the back window or bumper of their vehicle: Ranger Tab, Special Forces Tab, Parachutist Badge ("Jump Wings"), various unit insignias, Navy and Marine Corps Parachutist Insignia, Explosive Ordnance Disposal Badge, etc. Each of these devices represents a significant achievement and is a source of pride for the recipient and their family, but it may be best to consider not listing an entire resume on the back of a vehicle. If you are current or former military and this describes you, consider scraping off most of the stickers from your vehicle. A sticker indicating your branch of service might not be an issue, but a list of qualification badges is best avoided. Be the **GRAY MAN**.

—**Stickers about firearms and related topics.** Avoid putting stickers that show support or enthusiasm for gun manufacturers, particularly firearms, ammunition, or the Second Amendment, on your vehicle. In areas where support for the Second Amendment is lacking, there have been numerous examples of the police receiving an anonymous call where they were told "some guy in a vehicle with a gun sticker (specific details provided) on the rear window rolled down his driver's side window and brandished a handgun at me while sitting at a traffic light. Here is the make/model/license plate and the vehicle's direction of travel."

Although completely untrue, the story may be plausible enough for law enforcement authorities that they are required to follow up. A false complaint like this can result in difficulties for you until the situation is sorted out. This type of harassment can be effective and highly annoying. You may be targeted simply because you displayed a firearms-related sticker on the back of your car or truck, which indicated a high likelihood that you had a firearm in your vehicle. **AVOID, AVOID, AVOID.**

WHAT TO DO, WHAT NOT TO DO

Conflict on the Interstate

It was a beautiful Saturday morning, and Ron and Tori wanted to beat the crowd and get to the Outlet Mall down the highway just as it opened. They buckled their two small children into the car seats in the back of their four-door sedan and prepared to head out for the mall. Ron had been extremely busy all week with his military unit preparing for an upcoming inspection, and he was excited to spend some time together with Tori and the kids and relax a bit.

The family was driving along an Interstate Highway toward Washington, DC. Unbeknownst to them, a large protest march was planned for Saturday morning in downtown Washington due to a recent significant increase in the level of US military involvement in an ongoing overseas conflict. Protesters were heading to the march from across the entire region, with many arriving via the same Interstate Highway on which the family was currently driving.

An older van covered with a broad assortment of political bumper stickers was approaching the family's sedan on the Interstate from behind. The driver of the van was speeding and trying to get to the protest march on time. A colorful military bumper sticker on the back of the family's sedan caught his eye. He said to the other passengers, "Look at that sticker! He must be one of the military guys from that base we just passed back off the highway. Let's teach him a lesson!"

The other passengers enthusiastically agreed, and the driver rapidly maneuvered his vehicle alongside the family's sedan. Partially opening the van's sliding side door, one of the passengers in the back of the van hurled a brick into the side window of the sedan. The van's occupants laughed and sped away.

Ron and Tori were caught completely off-guard as the brick hit the window with a loud thump. The brick cracked the car window and caused severe damage but then bounced off. Fortunately, the window did not shatter, and the brick did not penetrate the vehicle. Startled by the sudden impact, Ron struggled to maintain control of the car at highway speeds.

He quickly regained his composure and pulled off onto the shoulder of the road, bringing the vehicle to a stop. The children were scared and crying; Ron and Tori were both trying to figure out what had just happened and why. The van and the brick thrower were long gone.

Ron reported the crime to the state troopers, but the perpetrators were never caught. Back at the military base, Ron reported the crime to his chain of command and the military police. Although not of the same magnitude, some other low-level incidents had occurred over the weekend to other service members. The local military installation commander ordered all personnel assigned to the base to immediately remove all military-related stickers from their personal vehicles until further notice and, in his words, "sterilize your cars."

WHAT TO DO, WHAT NOT TO DO:

Ron and Tori did not do anything wrong or seek direct conflict with their adversary. This story is a real-world example of the phrase, "Sometimes bad things happen to good people." Ron and Tori were minding their own business and just quietly living their life while serving the country. Unfortunately, they were victimized by unknown perpetrators simply for showing their pride as a military family. Considering the time frame when this circumstance happened and the strong feelings on both sides of the political issue, in hindsight, it would have been prudent to remove all stickers or emblems from the family car at an earlier time. It would have been better to **LIVE UNDER THE RADAR** and avoid trouble. Look at your vehicle and remove any stickers, military or otherwise, that might draw unwanted attention.

—**Window tinting.** Practice what is normal in a particular area to blend in. Dark window tinting is broadly seen on the roads in Florida and many southern states since it protects against damage from the strong sunlight and lessens the heat buildup in your vehicle's interior. Dark tint that allows only a specific, low percentage of light transmission is legal and commonplace in this region. In some northern states, any window tinting beyond what is standard equipment from the vehicle manufacturer may be illegal, especially on the driver and passenger side front windows. From a security perspective, dark window tinting can provide you with a high degree of anonymity and privacy while inside your vehicle. Simultaneously, it can decrease visibility during hours of darkness and make control of your vehicle substantially more difficult. Research the laws for your state of residence to ensure compliance, and then choose a balanced level of window tinting that protects you and your vehicle's interior from the sun's rays while not hindering your ability to drive at night.

In some states, undercover law enforcement agents and licensed private investigators are authorized to employ extremely dark tinting down to five percent light transmission, far exceeding the legal limit for regular civilians. The challenge with having such extremely dark tint is that it may actually cause these vehicles to stand out from the crowd since they may look different than what is normally allowed on the road. It could serve to highlight rather than conceal their presence when applied to windows in low-profile vehicles.

4) Interior preparation.

If someone walks up to your vehicle in a parking lot and looks into the windows, what will they see? Can they learn anything about you? The next time you park in a shopping center, casually glance into the vehicles adjacent to yours (in a non-alerting manner, of course, to avoid trouble). You will likely be amazed at the number of papers and other items carelessly left on the seats in plain view. Mail and packages with complete addresses, reports, credit card statements, pay stubs, books, documents, and work papers are examples of what other drivers will regularly leave fully exposed on the seats in their vehicles. Many people forget that once they park their vehicle and go into a store or their workplace, whatever is visible through the windows becomes fair game for information collection by a potential adversary.

When keeping papers in your vehicle, consider concealing them in a briefcase or backpack, and then place the bag into your car's trunk out of sight. **Hide everything.** It is even better to leave the bag at home and not store any papers or other personal information in your vehicle. **Goal: when an observer looks into your car from the outside, nothing of monetary or informational value should ever be visible.** You do not want an adversary to gain anything of value from a visual or physical search of your vehicle or to learn anything about you. **If someone searches your car, they should find nothing of interest** except the vehicle registration and insurance card. If you are truly committed and want to go the extra mile, keep these documents in a separate folder or portfolio along with your car keys. Remove this portfolio and your keys every time you leave your vehicle. If someone gains access to your vehicle in your absence, there will be no identifying paperwork of any type available for their immediate review.

5) Car keys.

Never store car keys inside your vehicle in any location, including the glove box or console; this includes while your car is parked in your driveway or even inside your locked garage at home. When exiting your vehicle, shut off the ignition and remove the keys. Keep the keys continuously on your body or store them in a secure storage location separate from the vehicle. **Do not leave your car running if more than a few feet away or when your attention is focused elsewhere.** Shut off your vehicle and remove the keys. Your car can be stolen in a flash if it is left running and you are distracted nearby. Small behaviors like this need to become ingrained habits and will lessen the chances of your vehicle being stolen.

This sounds like simple stuff, but it is surprising how complacent some people are when it comes to maintaining positive control over their car keys. This issue may be more noticeable if a person was raised in an environment where vehicle theft was uncommon. In the city, vehicle theft is an unfortunate reality of life and happens far too often. For your awareness, some insurance companies may not pay out on a claim if the keys were left inside your vehicle, enabling theft. Other companies may still cover the claim under a comprehensive policy. Research the details of your insurance policy to avoid an unwelcome surprise. Play it safe, and never leave your keys in your vehicle.

6) Approaching your vehicle.

Each time that you approach your vehicle when it has been out of your positive control, even if for just a few moments, it is wise to conduct a brief inspection to assess the current security status. This is especially true if your car was parked in a parking garage, parking lot, shopping center, or similar public location where it was not fully secured.

—**Inspect "big picture" items.** Approach your vehicle and examine it in a low-key, non-alerting manner to avoid drawing unwanted scrutiny from casual bystanders who may be in the vicinity. Rapidly look over the entire exterior condition. **Quickly and methodically glance over the entire car** from top to bottom, noting anything that grabs your immediate attention. Look for "big picture" items that catch your eye. Walk in a circle around the circumference of the car; this should only take perhaps fifteen to twenty seconds. Start with the roof of the car, including the sunroof (if present). Look for broken windows, damage to the door handles, smashed headlights or taillights, and flat tires. Is there anything around the tires that could puncture them, such as broken glass, nails, or even a caltrop? Are the license plates missing (stolen)? Is a foreign object shoved into the exhaust pipe blocking the exhaust flow? Does anything appear to be out of the ordinary? If the answer to any of these "big picture" items is yes, then investigate further. Observe anyone who is loitering in the area who may have been involved in sabotaging your vehicle.

If significant damage is visible, is it still possible to drive the car? For example, if the windshield is smashed, the car must be towed since it is illegal to drive with a broken windshield. If one or more of the tires have been slashed, be aware of who may be lurking nearby. Depending on your circumstances, some adversaries may slash a tire or just let the air out to cause deflation, forcing you to change the tire in a setting that may be advantageous for their purposes. While changing a tire, you will be distracted by the task at hand, which can allow an adversary to easily gain access to you on their terms.

Plan ahead and join a travel club that provides twenty-four-hour tire changing and towing services. When you observe a tire that has been deflated or slashed, and you are in an isolated parking garage or on a quiet, dark side street, immediately leave the area and go to a secure location in a nearby business or **HARD POINT**. Contact the travel club and arrange to have one of their service providers either change the tire with the vehicle's spare tire or tow the vehicle if necessary. This **limits your exposure**. These services are also available through most automobile insurance policies for a small fee.

LOOK TWICE TIP

Caltrops

A caltrop (also known as a calthrop) is a metal tire deflation device that can be quickly placed or thrown on the ground to temporarily deny a wheeled vehicle from driving through an area. Each device has multiple metal points (usually four), and no matter how it is placed on the ground, one of the points will always face upward. The devices are made of a very strong metal.

Caltrops may be placed underneath a stationary or parked vehicle's tires so that once the vehicle is put into motion and rolls forward or backward, the caltrops will immediately puncture the tires, causing a massive failure. Caltrops may be used individually, or multiple devices may be employed simultaneously.

Alternately, numerous caltrops can be thrown across a pathway or section of a road to deny passage by vehicles equipped with standard pneumatic tires. Vehicles with run-flat tires would arguably be much less affected since the tire would not immediately blow out.

When approaching your vehicle, glance at the front and back of the tires to ensure that broken glass, nails, and devices like caltrops are not present.

7) Detailed inspection.

If your security situation is heightened due to extreme personal circumstances, it may be prudent to conduct a detailed, methodical inspection. This would be appropriate if an adversary may have tampered with your vehicle while it was not under your positive control. A detailed inspection will take some time and requires a flashlight.

Prior to experiencing a real-world requirement to inspect your vehicle, take the time to thoroughly look over your car and learn what is normal. Open the hood and study the engine and other components in the engine compartment. **Goal: Learn what "normal" looks like so that you can quickly find an IMPROVISED EXPLOSIVE DEVICE (IED) placed anywhere on the vehicle or identify any major parts or equipment that have been sabotaged.** Next, lie prone on the ground and, using a flashlight, look underneath the vehicle at the undercarriage to assess what "normal" looks like; if you can, slide under the vehicle on your back to get the best view. Finally, open your trunk and look at your spare tire compartment, examining the spare tire and car jack. Throughout this process, take pictures on your mobile device in case you need a ready reference to assist your memory and recall what "normal" looks like for the vehicle. These photos can be used for comparison if something looks out of place in the future.

Remove everything from the vehicle that is not necessary, including all of the "stuff" many people collect in their vehicles over time. Store all of these items someplace away from the vehicle. When facing a significant threat, consider permanently removing all of the floor and trunk mats in advance to speed up inspections and lessen hiding places for an adversary to exploit. Under the most severe circumstances, permanently remove all carpeting down to the bare floorboard.

To conduct a detailed inspection, perform an initial review and slowly walk around the exterior of the car. Inspect for anything **significant** that is out of the ordinary. If the car is dirty, look for handprints or smudges near the door handles or on the hood or trunk, which may indicate that someone was attempting to gain access to the interior portions of the vehicle. A clean car without any dust or dirt makes it harder to spot these signs. **In extreme situations, it may be better to allow a vehicle to remain dirty as an aid for detecting tampering.**

Look for visible wires on the exterior of the vehicle from either the taillight running into the trunk or under the gas hatch cover. Both of these could point to the presence of an explosive device in one of these areas. The taillights offer a potential source of power for the detonation of an explosive device. If wires like this are found, immediately depart the area and contact the authorities for assistance.

Get underneath the vehicle with a flashlight and examine the undercarriage, looking for nefarious objects or tampering. Pay close attention to the tires, wheels, axles, and foreign objects in the exhaust pipe or pipes, depending on the model of the car. Look for any significant amount of fluid on the ground under the vehicle. If there are pools of fluid on the ground, search for their source to determine if any lines have been cut.

Go to the driver's door and observe inside the vehicle through the window. Look for things that are out of the ordinary. Is something out of place, or has anything obviously been moved or tampered with? Carefully and slowly, begin opening the door, examining the door jamb for anything that is alerting. Cautiously open the door and leave it wide open. Look around the accelerator and brake pedals to ensure they appear sound and untouched. Using your flashlight, examine under the driver's seat. Glance over the steering wheel and controls. Observe the vehicle's other doors from inside the car to see if anything appears out of place. Repeat this procedure for each of the other car doors from the outside.

Inspect the engine compartment, which is generally located under the front hood, depending on the model of the vehicle. Pull the hood release from within the vehicle cabin. Move to the front of the car and open the hood slowly and with great care, observing if anything appears to be of concern. Slowly lift the hood and secure it in the fully open position. Examine the engine compartment, searching for any obvious tampering or the inclusion of an explosive device of some type. If something appears to be out of place, it warrants additional investigation. Pay special attention to any nefarious objects along the wall of the engine compartment located in close proximity to the vehicle cabin. This is a likely location where an adversary could place a device designed to explode toward the passengers inside a vehicle. A device hidden in this portion of the engine compartment is not visible to passengers, and any explosion would not be lessened or hindered by the engine.

Move to the rear of the vehicle and cautiously open the

trunk, observing if anything appears to be of concern. Slowly raise the trunk to its fully open position. Examine the interior of the trunk for anything out of the ordinary. Methodically and carefully examine the spare tire compartment, the spare tire, and the jack for anything out of the ordinary.

This completes the detailed inspection. Add or delete inspection items as necessary, depending on your circumstances and type of vehicle.

8) Enter the vehicle.

Below are several things you should do upon entering a vehicle.

—Open the vehicle door and sit in the car seat; IMMEDIATELY lock the vehicle. This is the very first thing that should be done prior to anything else. Many people sit in a vehicle and are promptly distracted by a range of other things, most of which cause them to look down or away from the car door. This is the perfect time for an adversary to approach the vehicle and gain access to you while you are distracted and at a disadvantage. It is also the ideal time to steal the vehicle because the car keys are present, and the vehicle may even be turned on. All a criminal has to do is physically remove you or force you to exit the car, and it is theirs for the taking. Immediately locking a vehicle's doors upon entering provides a layer of security and makes an adversary's job harder. Some cars have a mechanism that automatically locks all of the vehicle's doors after a certain speed is reached; depending on the vehicle model, this may be roughly nine miles per hour. Do not simply rely on this mechanism to lock the doors, but instead, make it a habit to lock the doors on your own immediately upon entering the car.

When picking someone up in a vehicle, remember that the vehicle doors will likely be locked. It is a common error to pull alongside a curb, and the person waiting for pickup tugs on the door handle only to find it is still locked. This is inefficient and does not build confidence in the person who is waiting. Instead, to conduct a pickup smoothly and efficiently, unlock the doors a few seconds prior to pulling over to the curb. The individual waiting on the curb can open the door on the first attempt and quickly enter the vehicle. While smoothly driving away from the curb, immediately lock the doors again.

—**When carrying a handbag, place it on the floor in front of the passenger seat.** This lessens the visibility of the handbag to someone walking by the vehicle while waiting at a traffic signal. If a criminal smashes a car window at a traffic light to grab the bag, it is harder to reach if placed on the floor. Consider draping a towel or jacket over the bag to conceal its presence while in the vehicle.

—**Keep the vehicle's windows fully closed at all times.** If the interior temperature of the vehicle gets too hot, turn on the air conditioner. If the air is stuffy, turn up the blower fan speed. Even though an adversary can break the windows with a window breaker tool or a blunt object, the windows still provide an additional layer of security and slow an adversary down. Keep the windows in the "up" position (fully closed) at all times unless paying a toll in cash at a toll booth or some similar activity.

—**Disable the feature that automatically turns on a vehicle's interior lights.** Interior cabin lights (including the main "dome light") automatically turn on in most vehicles when one of the doors is opened or the vehicle is unlocked. This provides passengers with a degree of illumination for convenience and safety when entering or exiting a vehicle. The lighting also temporarily degrades or ruins night vision and illuminates passengers, which is not desirable if an adversary may be observing from a distance. Instead, consider disabling this feature so that when the vehicle is unlocked or the doors are opened, the interior vehicle light remains off. Master the art of moving in the dark.

—**Learn to operate the vehicle's controls.** Spend the necessary time to learn how to operate all of your vehicle's controls in a smooth and efficient manner. Know how to manage every feature during the day and in complete darkness at night without requiring focused thought. These skills must become second nature. When renting a vehicle, take a few moments to learn how to effectively manipulate any essential knobs, switches, and levers to ensure smooth use even while under pressure. Your skill with the controls may not be second nature like in your personal vehicle, but ensure you develop the ability to easily turn on the headlights, adjust the mirrors, defog the windows, and lock the doors, among other key tasks.

—**Never use the parking brake.** When jumping into your car and departing rapidly during a stressful situation, it is easy to forget to disengage the parking brake. This can damage the brakes and hinder a quick escape. **It is best to never use your vehicle's parking brake.** If you only apply your parking brake every now and then, you are unlikely to develop a consistent habit of releasing the parking brake every time you enter your vehicle. Releasing the parking brake is just one more thing to think about when getting into your car, and it is an unnecessary waste of time. A possible exception may be if you live in an extremely hilly area and you consistently use your parking brake each day to prevent your vehicle from rolling down hills while parked. Otherwise, turn the wheels so that your car will roll into the curb if parked on a hill, which stops all motion.

—**Wear your seat belt.** Always wear a seat belt since it serves multiple purposes. Seat belts provide effective restraint during an accident and are essential to keeping all passengers alive, including those in the back seat. During high-performance driving, a seat belt keeps you correctly placed in the seat to maximize your control of the vehicle, especially when engaged in high-speed cornering. Seat belts also keep you and other passengers in the proper location to lessen or eliminate injuries if airbags are deployed during a collision.

LOOK TWICE TIP

How to Quickly Release a Seat Belt

When wearing a seat belt and trying to exit a vehicle under great stress, it can be exceedingly difficult and slow to locate and release the seat belt locking mechanism. This task is made even harder because of the degraded fine motor skills caused by adrenaline surging through your body.

To quickly release the seat belt, grab the top of the seat belt by the retractor mounted to the car side wall near your head, and then run your hand all the way down the belt to the release button. Press the release button and exit the vehicle. This is much faster than fumbling around looking for the release button and is also effective in the dark.

9) Hand position on the steering wheel.

Place your hands at the nine o'clock and three o'clock positions on the steering wheel or as close to this as the steering wheel design will allow. Some steering wheels have hand cut-outs located closer to the eight o'clock and four o'clock positions. If this is the case, use these hand cut-outs when grasping the steering wheel. You may see other drivers with their hands bunched closely together at the top of the steering wheel. This is a sure sign that they do not know much about performance driving; no one driving with this hand position can effectively control the steering wheel while aggressively turning or trying to avoid an accident. When the hands are bunched closely together, your range of motion with the steering wheel is severely limited. There is also a risk of broken bones if the airbag forcibly deploys and your hands are placed at the ten o'clock and two o'clock positions or higher toward the top of the wheel.

Place your thumbs straight up the sides of the steering wheel and grasp the wheel only with your fingers and palms. Do not hook your thumbs on the steering wheel. This hand position affords maximum control and "feel" of the steering wheel while driving.

While driving under low-stress conditions with few or no other vehicles in close proximity, it is optional to hold the steering wheel with only one hand at the six o'clock position. This is a resting position that may be suitable for longer trips on an Interstate Highway, for example. While using this technique, your reaction time and ability to respond will be decreased.

You might like to install a steering wheel cover to add "bling" to your vehicle. Some of these covers feature rhinestones, faux wool, or other fancy upgrades to really make your car stand out from others. Avoid all of these steering wheel covers because they may degrade the solid contact between your hands and the steering wheel surface, resulting in a loss of control when steering under challenging circumstances. Skip the steering wheel cover and save the money.

10) Seat placement.

You will often see other drivers position the driver's seat far too close to the steering wheel, with some even placing the seat only inches from the steering column. This can be dangerous. Watch a video of an airbag deployment to quickly understand why it is best for you to position your seat much further back from the steering wheel. **To determine the correct distance, place your wrists just over the top of the steering wheel, ensuring a slight bend in your elbows. Grasp the steering wheel from this location. Adjust your seat to allow for pushing the brake pedal all the way to the floor with a slight bend in the knee.** This is a good driving position based on body geometry and will allow effective control of the steering wheel and full manipulation of the brake pedal. It will also maintain an advantageous position in relation to the airbag located in the steering column. Raise or lower your seat height to afford the best possible view through the front windshield. Adjust the interior rearview and side-view mirrors to maximize visibility around the exterior of the vehicle.

11) Distractions inside your vehicle.

Maintain focus and eliminate distractions when you are driving. Even though you may truly believe you are endowed with an uncanny ability to juggle multiple complex activities simultaneously without any errors or any degradation of your high-performance driving skills, science tells us you are probably overestimating your abilities. A lot. To best improve everyday security, **do not text and drive. Do not scroll through social media.** Save the texting for later once you have pulled over your vehicle along the side of the road or are parked in a safe location. A quick way to experience road rage is to cause a vehicle accident because you were texting while driving. Depending on who the other party is, this type of situation could degrade rapidly because it was likely avoidable.

When faced with a threatening situation, **turn off the vehicle's radio.** Music or other sound can be a major distraction and limit your ability to hear and concentrate while dealing with the immediate danger and attaining a positive outcome. By way of example, when driving in extremely dangerous war zones overseas, the car stereo was never on. The danger was real, and instead of listening to a steady selection of the latest Top 40 hits, the driver needed to focus completely on dealing with the threats at hand. Whether in a threat situation or facing challenging conditions such as a snowstorm or pounding rain, the best advice is to **JUST DRIVE** and turn off the radio.

12) Hitchhikers.

Never pick up hitchhikers, whether male or female. Their appearance does not matter. The hitchhiker may appear to be the nicest, kindest, most modestly dressed person in the world. After stopping and allowing a hitchhiker into the vehicle, you have given up your **PERSONAL SPACE,** and you can be attacked without warning and will have limited ability to effectively react to the threat. Even if no attack occurs and the hitchhiker is dropped off without incident at their destination, this is an unknown person who could later make false statements about you and your conduct to the authorities. **AVOID, AVOID, AVOID.** Do not pick up hitchhikers.

13) Broken-down cars and minor accidents.

Be wary of someone who appears to have a broken-down car alongside the road or who appears to have been in a minor accident. There are numerous examples of these situations being a setup. A helpful and considerate citizen offers assistance to the people who appear to be down on their luck alongside the road only to be attacked, robbed, and possibly have their vehicle stolen. Some of these kind citizens have even been killed when stopping to offer assistance. Even though you may want to be helpful, do not stop to offer help. Times have unfortunately changed, and once stopped, you are **EXPOSED TO RISK**. Unless you personally know the individuals involved, it is better to **MITIGATE RISK** and call law enforcement to respond to the situation. Continue driving and know that you have reported the situation and done your part to assist your fellow motorists.

If you are in a minor accident while driving a vehicle, ensure to pay close attention to the surroundings. Did someone bump into your car at a stop sign or traffic light? Does something not feel right about the situation? Some criminals may "bump" into your car at very low speeds, knowing that you will exit the vehicle to survey the damage and talk with the other driver about the accident. After exiting your vehicle, the criminals use this opportunity to steal your car, possibly robbing and harming you along the way. If involved in a minor accident and you are not comfortable with stopping your vehicle for any of a multitude of reasons, consider driving directly to the nearest police station to report the mishap. While driving to the police station, call 9-1-1, tell the dispatcher about the accident, why you were uncomfortable with stopping at the scene, and that you are driving directly to the police station while on the phone. Follow the dispatcher's guidance. If you are comfortable with the situation, then stop your vehicle and interact with the other driver as normal. This is a judgment call.

14) Speed.

Carefully monitor speed when driving. You may judge that higher speeds can limit your exposure time in dangerous areas or sections of a route and, therefore, increase your security. **IT DEPENDS**. It is certain that increased speed makes it more difficult to detect threats and respond properly. While trying to pay attention and determine if someone is following you (or possibly leading you or running parallel to you on an adjacent street), speedy driving may make your task much tougher. Once a threat has been identified, speed can be useful for evading that threat to a point. Be careful because as speed increases, it becomes much more difficult to control your vehicle safely and effectively. The chances of causing an accident involving injury or severe vehicle damage go up substantially as the speed increases.

15) Parking.

Carefully choose where you park. It is always useful to know the environment and have a **BASELINE** for the intended parking area. Are there a lot of "smash and grab" crimes in the location, where criminals break the windows of parked cars and steal whatever items of value they can grab? Have there been a significant number of vehicle thefts reported in the vicinity? Having an awareness of what goes on in a particular neighborhood can assist you in selecting the best parking location. Some things to look for when choosing a parking spot include ample lighting, security cameras, the presence of nearby law enforcement officers or security guards, and security fencing around the parking garage or lot. Are there a significant number of people loitering in the area? Once you leave your vehicle and walk away, these folks may get busy with your vehicle for their nefarious purposes. Pay close attention to the surroundings.

When parking in a parking space, you can either pull into the spot with the front of the car (headfirst) or back in with the rear of the car. Backing in is also called **TACTICAL PARKING**. The benefit of tactical parking is that it offers greater control, and once the car is parked, it is much easier to rapidly depart from the parking spot by pulling forward into the traffic flow. Tactical parking allows for better observation of the front and sides while exiting the parking spot. Some city parking lots dictate how drivers must park. Many lots will only allow headfirst parking and prohibit tactical parking. If you choose to violate the parking lot rules, you may find that your vehicle was towed away at your expense while you were away from the lot. If offered the option, tactical parking is preferable and safer.

16) Clock system for traffic circles.

When describing the movement of a vehicle through a traffic circle, picture the traffic circle as the face of an analog clock. **Upon entering the traffic circle**, twelve o'clock is straight ahead. Enter the traffic circle at the six o'clock position on the clock face. To describe where to exit the traffic circle if there are multiple exits, simply say "exit one o'clock" or "exit ten o'clock" to correspond to the appropriate exit on the clock face (the traffic circle). This simple system eliminates confusion when communicating with others, especially if you have a passenger in your vehicle who is navigating or providing directions and you are just following the passenger's instructions.

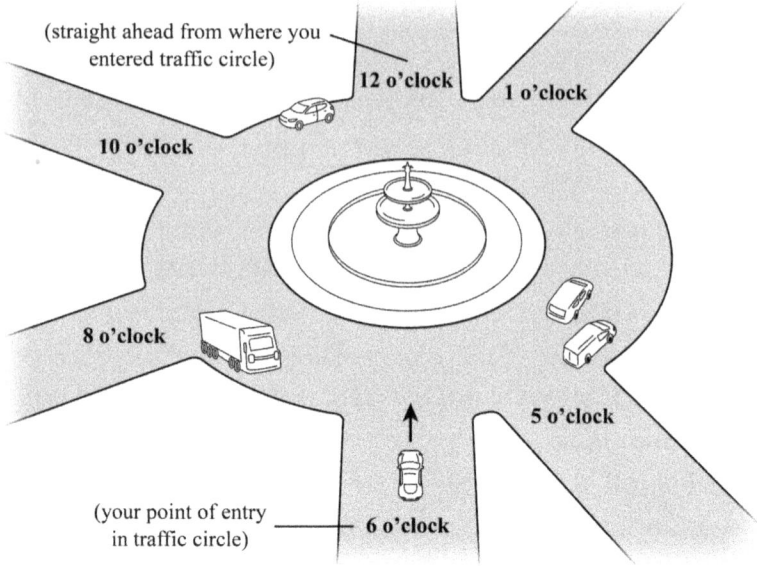

(straight ahead from where you entered traffic circle)

12 o'clock

1 o'clock

10 o'clock

8 o'clock

5 o'clock

(your point of entry in traffic circle)

6 o'clock

Clock system for traffic circles.

17) Clock System for contact.

Use a similar system when discussing any movement of your vehicle and also to quickly alert others in the vehicle to an incoming threat or attack. As you sit in the vehicle facing to the front, the following always applies:

- Front of vehicle: twelve o'clock
- Right-side door: three o'clock
- Rear of vehicle: six o'clock
- Left-side door: nine o'clock

For example, if a threat or attack is coming from eleven o'clock toward your vehicle, say, "contact eleven o'clock." Everyone in the vehicle now knows where to look and can prepare to take action. If a threat is coming from seven o'clock, say, "contact seven o'clock."

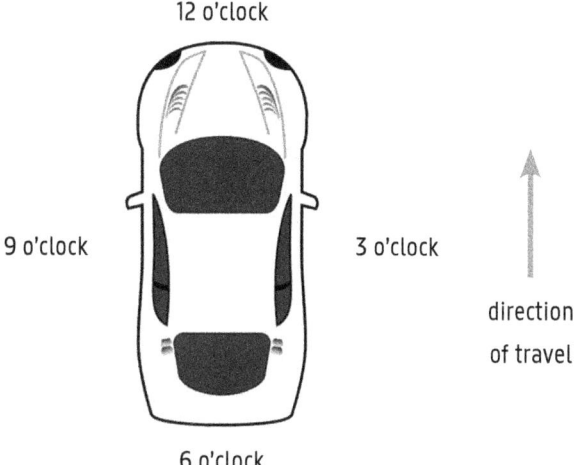

12 o'clock

9 o'clock 3 o'clock

direction
of travel

6 o'clock

Clock system for "contact" while in a vehicle.

The same applies if you see an approaching car accident but cannot maneuver out of the way. For example, say, "brace for impact, ten o'clock." This may provide a second or two for passengers to brace themselves before the car is hit or strikes another object.

18) Attacks.

When attacked, the rules change, and the situation immediately becomes a fight to protect yourself and your loved ones. For the moment, nothing else matters.

—**Everything becomes a road.** When attacked while driving a vehicle, remember that roads are just guidelines for driving. **If you are facing a lethal threat and need to escape**, the only available escape route may force you to leave the road. Under these circumstances, it may be necessary to consider driving on the shoulder of a highway, on the median, on sidewalks, through a grassy field or someone's yard, or even through a park. When trying to escape, everything becomes a road. This course of action is only for the worst of circumstances where your life is in jeopardy. It is critical to avoid hitting pedestrians or other drivers or causing a deadly accident in your efforts to save your own life and escape. Control your speed, but continue to move until reaching safety. **Always have an escape route while driving**.

—**Back up.** Sometimes, it may be necessary to back out of trouble, and your vehicle cannot be driven forward. There are increased risks with backing up, especially with front-wheel-drive vehicles. It can be difficult to maintain full control of the steering when traveling backward. To back up successfully, watch where the vehicle is headed by looking in the rearview mirror, looking over your shoulder, or in the side-view mirror. Be careful because driving in reverse requires some skill.

—**Steering is more important than braking**. If necessary, "aim" your car by controlling the steering. Use the brakes to "dump energy" while moving. Never ride the brakes.

—**To avoid hitting an object, do not look at it.** When you were a child playing baseball or softball, a coach may have told you, "Keep your eye on the ball all the way from the pitcher's hand until you hit it with your bat." This is good advice because while staring at something, the chances of hitting it go up significantly. The same logic applies when trying to AVOID hitting an object with your vehicle, like a car bumper in front of you or a solid object you want to pass by. While maneuvering a vehicle, do not stare at an object that you wish to avoid hitting, or you will likely have an unwelcome surprise. Instead, **LOOK AND DRIVE TOWARD WHERE YOU WANT TO**

GO, and you will be far more likely to miss hitting the object you wish to avoid.

—**Removal from the vehicle.** If an attacker blocks or stops your automobile and then attempts to remove you from the vehicle by force, this is a sign that the attacker wants you alive, at least for now. This could be a "kidnapping for ransom," or the attacker may want you for some other nefarious purpose. If the attacker wanted you dead, they would just kill you on the spot instead of trying to take you away to another location. If an attacker grabs you and tries to bring you to another place, this is not good. Your attacker is removing you from a chaotic situation that is not well-controlled and taking you to a location that the attacker has likely prepared in advance for this moment. You do not want to go to this place. It is a personal choice, but fight like your life depends on it, and do not go willingly with the attacker.

—**Your automobile is a weapon.** If an attacker presents a lethal threat, such as pointing a firearm toward you through the windshield, keep in mind that your vehicle is a weapon. **You can control the threat by rapidly accelerating your vehicle through your attacker.** Press your accelerator to the floorboard and aim your car directly at the attacker. This may be a necessary action to preserve your life.

When driving a standard vehicle, the engine is in front of the vehicle cabin under the hood and will provide a significant amount of **COVER** from gunfire. Crouch down inside the vehicle to the best of your ability while maintaining some limited observation of the attacker and where your vehicle is heading. Limit your body's exposure as much as possible; any part of your body that is above the heavy engine block runs the risk of being hit by gunfire. When driving a mid-engine or rear-engine vehicle, this technique can still be employed but without the protection of the engine block since the engine is located behind the vehicle cabin.

This is a lethal force technique only to be used in a situation where you are facing the threat of lethal force from an attacker and where you fear for your life or those of your loved ones.

—**Escaping from a vehicle in an attack.** If your vehicle is immobilized or blocked and you are not able to escape an ongoing attack by fleeing the scene in your car, you may be forced to rapidly get out of the vehicle and attempt to **GET OFF THE X.** If possible, **exit the vehicle on the opposite of side of where the attacker is located**. Run away if you can. If unable to run away, keep the vehicle between you and the attacker. This may allow you to communicate with your adversary and buy time to de-escalate the situation. Depending on what caused the attack, such as road rage or a vehicle accident, this may also allow time for your attacker to calm down.

If the attacker is engaging you with gunfire, use the engine block (remember where it is located in your car model) or the wheels to provide **COVER** from the effects of gunfire. The wheels are made of strong metal and can provide protection from bullets.

—**"COVER will not remain cover for long."** If you stay in one position for more than a few seconds, your attacker will often maneuver to a better position where they can reengage you with their weapon. Use available cover until you can quickly move to a better location and escape. If you have your own firearm and engage the attacker, **do not "crowd cover."** Stay back approximately three feet from the vehicle, crouched behind the engine block or the wheels while you engage the attacker. If you are too close to the car or are leaning over the hood or trunk to provide support for your arms while shooting, any incoming rounds may travel along the surface of the vehicle and ricochet up into your upper body or head, causing significant injury or death.

—**Do not hide behind car doors.** Unlike what you may have been conditioned to believe through television and movies, bullets fired from both rifles and many handguns easily travel through car doors. Doors do not provide effective **COVER**. They only provide **CONCEALMENT** from observation.

SUBWAY

Many major cities, such as New York, Atlanta, Chicago, and Washington, D.C., among others, have well-developed subway systems. Various portions of these systems may be below ground level, at ground level, or even above ground, depending on the city. It is smart to stay current with all of the local news about what is going on in your city's subway system. Is crime a major problem? What types of crimes have been reported in recent weeks or months? By gaining a detailed understanding of the **PROBABLE** threats that you may face in your local subway system, you will be better positioned to tailor any preparations or responses to improve your everyday security.

1) Learn the "big picture" of the subway system.

If you plan to ride the subway frequently, gain a full appreciation and understanding of your city's subway system. Obtain a physical map from one of the subway stations or find a digital map online. Study the subway lines that you will use regularly and learn the names of each of the stops in sequential order.

If you ride the subway frequently, this will occur naturally due to your everyday exposure. Learn where the different lines connect to one another and where the major transfer stations are located. If you miss a stop and have to reroute, this information will be important to know. When on the train, stay aware of your current location along the line at all times in case the security situation degrades and you have to exit the subway car at the next stop. Know the standard procedures associated with riding the subway in your city to avoid causing an issue with other riders and drawing attention to yourself. Pay attention to announcements about delays, closures, track repair, platform improvement projects, and other work that may affect your routing and impact your security.

2) Learn about the specific stops where you embark and debark from trains.

It is essential to gain a complete understanding of the specific stops where you get on and off the train. Although security situations certainly can happen inside subway cars while the train is moving, a large number of security incidents occur while waiting at a subway station. Criminals may prefer to commit their crimes when they are able to run off of the subway platform and disappear into the open city streets instead of having to wait in the confines of a moving train until the next stop to disembark and escape.

—**Entrances and exits.** Know how to quickly and efficiently get in and out of the subway station through all entrances and exits. Learn where each exit opens out onto the street to allow for immediate orientation to your surroundings following departure from the subway station.

—**Escalators, elevators, and stairs.** Identify where each of these elements is located in the station. Are the elevators consistently in service or often out of order? Are multiple escalators or stairways present?

—**Emergency assistance.** Know how to get help in case of an emergency. Is there a regular security or police presence assigned to the station? Where can these authorities be found, or are they constantly patrolling throughout the station? How many officers are present, and during what hours? If security is provided by security guards rather than law enforcement, are they armed with firearms, or do they only carry radios? If no security or police are regularly assigned to the station, where are the duress alarms located? How do you call for help?

—**Specific issues.** Have there been any consistent problems at your primary stations? Have your primary stations been a hotbed for crime? Are there any specific issues, such as gang activity?

3) Analysis of the subway platform.

Upon entering the subway platform, quickly scan across the entire area for a few seconds and look for anything or anyone that catches your eye as an immediate threat. This is where it is essential to have a good **BASELINE,** so you know quickly if something is out of the ordinary or of potential concern.

Is someone acting in a bizarre manner, perhaps frightening other passengers? **Displays of mental illness** are a regular concern on many subway platforms and in subway cars. Avoid all interactions and maintain as much distance as possible. If someone is mentally ill, any contact can be unpredictable and quickly turn into a physical threat.

After this quick initial scan, mentally apply the **TRAFFIC LIGHT SYSTEM** to assess each person who is visible on the platform. If an individual or a group of people appear to be a potential threat, maintain distance, and once the train arrives, choose to enter a different subway car to avoid any interaction.

Stay in populated areas of the platform, preferably with your back to a wall so no one can get behind you; this allows you to limit your field of observation to 180 degrees. Standing with your back to a wall also keeps you well away from the tracks and **eliminates the opportunity for anyone to push you onto the train tracks.** There has been a disturbing trend of individuals being pushed onto the tracks in front of arriving trains, resulting in their deaths. Many of these individuals did not even know their attacker, and the violence was often completely random.

Do not get separated from other passengers or isolate yourself at one end of the platform. Depending on the volume of people present, seek to maintain your **PERSONAL SPACE** to avoid pickpockets, purse snatchers, and the like. Maintain good observation over the entrance to the platform so that you are immediately aware of who is coming and going. This helps to avoid surprise and provides the maximum opportunity to react to a threat as soon as it presents itself.

Violence on subways can happen at any time, including rush hour. It is generally smart, however, to use extra caution at times of heightened concern and, if possible, **AVOID** riding the subway during late night and early morning hours (such as 2:00 a.m.) when crime is at its peak. A review of your city's newspaper will often reveal crime statistics that spike during these time periods. Alcohol is frequently a contributing factor. Crimes on subway platforms and in subway cars can include physical attacks, robberies, indecent exposure, and even sexual assaults in some major cities. Carefully choose the times that you ride and maintain awareness. **Keep to yourself as much as possible,** and do not engage with other passengers. Avoid direct eye contact. When possible, ride the subway with family, friends, classmates, or co-workers and stay in a group.

4) Analysis of subway cars.

After boarding a train, immediately assess each of the passengers riding in the same car. **First,** glance across the entire subway car and see if anyone or anything immediately stands out as a potential threat; this should take just a couple of seconds. **Second,** take a few moments to mentally apply the **TRAFFIC LIGHT SYSTEM** to sort through the passengers, one by one, in a more methodical and detailed fashion. It is essential to have a good **BASELINE** for what is normal and what is unusual to assist in assessing any possible threats. Also, some subway systems have seats that face forward or backward in the car. When sitting in one of these seats, ensure awareness of who is sitting behind you to avoid an unwelcome surprise. **Third,** closely monitor who exits the car and, most importantly, who enters at each stop. If sitting or standing near an exit door and an individual or group enters the car and appears to be a threat, attempt to slip out of the car and onto the platform before the doors close and take the next train that arrives at the station. This is one of the reasons why it is important to maintain awareness and always know where you are located along the subway line.

MOTORCYCLES AND SCOOTERS

Let us take a look at some of the advantages and disadvantages of motorcycles and scooters, along with some security thoughts about both platforms.

Motorcycles have tremendous acceleration, are easy to maneuver, and, depending on the bike, may offer an efficient way to get around town but with a smaller footprint than an automobile. If you want to live **UNDER THE RADAR**, a motorcycle may be a good choice. If you purchase a highly stylish "big bike" from one of the well-known manufacturers, your motorcycle will likely draw significant attention on the roads, at traffic lights, and even when parked. Many of these big bikes are outfitted with drag pipes or other loud exhaust systems that generate even more attention. Extravagant, beautiful bikes are a pleasure to ride, but they fall outside the spectrum of interest for this text.

Instead, consider a medium-sized motorcycle that has ample engine horsepower while offering you the ability to blend into the local traffic environment more readily. This kind of bike offers quick speed and a lot of power, but not every head will turn as you drive by. Bright paint colors and lots of flashy details are best avoided. Forego the loud, attention-getting, high-performance exhaust system. By selecting

a less attention-grabbing motorcycle, you will end up with a low-footprint bike that sips gasoline, is relatively cheap to operate, easy to park, and, most importantly, will have excellent mobility.

A medium-sized motorcycle is capable of nimble movement around town and through traffic. If you are followed or actively pursued by an adversary in a car, this type of motorcycle offers you the ability to ride between two lanes of traffic along the dividing stripe when the traffic is slow-moving or at a standstill. This technique is known as "whitelining," or lane splitting, and allows you to quickly **BREAK CONTACT** from an adversary since it is unlikely that a four-wheeled vehicle of any type would be able to follow a motorcycle under these conditions. The shoulder of the road, no matter how narrow, may also provide an alternate route for your motorcycle when needed. The high acceleration of a motorcycle allows you to speed away swiftly after breaking out of dense traffic.

The downside with motorcycles is that they only have two wheels, so it is much easier for your bike to fall over or for you to lose control due to poor road conditions, rider error, or if your bike is struck by another vehicle. Most of the time, you will need to keep both hands on the handlebars. It can be difficult to safely ride through traffic if you need to remove one hand from the handlebars to manipulate a GPS receiver or conduct any other task. Motorcycles have much less overall protection than cars. Sometimes, it is harder for others to see you or your motorcycle, which may be good or bad, depending on the circumstances. Motorcycles are great in warmer climates but may be less effective in colder areas, especially during winter months when snow and ice prohibit safe or comfortable riding.

If you desire to be the **GRAY MAN**, it is far easier to conceal your identity on a motorcycle than in most automobiles or trucks. Carefully select a full-face helmet in a solid color. Combined with a dark-tinted visor and subdued clothing, it can be difficult to confirm your identity while you are on the road.

Like any vehicle, make sure to carefully look over your bike if it has been parked on the street or left for a period of time in a nonsecure location. It is important to ensure that nothing has been removed from the bike or altered and that no foreign object has been shoved into the chain or wheels, hindering their free movement. Look at the tires to confirm proper inflation and serviceability. If an adversary tampers with a motorcycle, the aftermath may be far more damaging than what would be experienced with an automobile or a truck. Motorcycle sabotage may even be lethal if the damage causes a crash while the rider is traveling at high speed.

Scooters, specifically sit-down scooters, are similar to motorcycles in appearance. They generally have smaller engines and smaller wheels, and most do not require you to shift gears. Scooters are designed for **ease of operation and control, and most are comfortable for a wide range of riders**. Many of the previous comments about motorcycles still apply, but a major difference is the rate of acceleration. A scooter is not capable of accelerating as quickly as a medium-sized motorcycle; it simply does not have as much power due to its smaller engine size. A scooter will also not reach the same top speed as a motorcycle. From a security perspective, the significant reduction in acceleration and speed offered by a scooter gives up some of the key advantages that a motorcycle enjoys over most automobiles and trucks. If you are being chased by an adversary in a car, it will be harder to escape on a scooter than if you were riding a motorcycle. You must rely more heavily on your scooter's greater maneuverability and smaller footprint to evade an adversary pursuing you in a car.

ELECTRIC SCOOTERS

Electric scooters, specifically standing scooters or **e-scooters**, are a relatively new technology that has tremendous capability and promise for some of the purposes discussed in this book. E-scooters are technically referred to as "motorized micromobility devices." Lightweight, fast, and affordable, many of these vehicles are capable of carrying a rider for up to forty miles on a single charge at approximately fifteen to thirty miles per hour. For a higher price, e-scooters are available that can easily carry a rider up substantial hills, with some vehicles achieving speeds of forty-five miles per hour. The highest-end models can even achieve seventy-five miles per hour but at a much greater investment and a substantial increase in weight. E-scooters are a superior vehicle for university campuses, paved paths, side streets with reduced traffic, and moving about a city with speed and a very small footprint.

From a security perspective, an e-scooter can help you move about town **UNDER THE RADAR**, with little to no

noise. Upon reaching your travel destination, simply fold up the e-scooter, pick it up, and carry the vehicle with you to a safe and secure indoor location. This eliminates any opportunity for an adversary to access your e-scooter. There is no need to leave it on the sidewalk or in a parking garage or parking lot. It goes wherever you go. The sheer portability of the vehicle is a significant advantage over other forms of transportation and helps to protect your e-scooter from tampering or theft.

Although an e-scooter allows you effortless movement around town with a minimal footprint, you run the risk of not being seen by other larger, faster-moving vehicles. This is of greatest concern at night since it may be harder for other drivers to see you and your e-scooter under cover of darkness. Some of the better-quality e-scooters have headlights, taillights, and turning signals, which may provide limited assistance to help others see your vehicle. The inability of other drivers to easily spot your e-scooter can be a significant advantage in certain security scenarios, but it can also be a disadvantage from a safety perspective.

E-scooters may prove hazardous when ridden over poorly maintained sidewalks, roads, or under wet conditions. If a high-speed model is selected, you may wish to consider wearing a helmet since the greater speeds also increase your chances of significant injury or death. These vehicles truly shine in climates where the average temperatures are consistently warm, such as Southern California or South Florida, since the weather affords an unlimited opportunity for year-round riding with fewer restrictions.

If you plan to rely on an e-scooter as a primary means of transportation or for any security scenario where you must keep a low profile, **it is best to purchase your own e-scooter instead of relying on a rental vehicle** found on the street in your city. By owning an e-scooter, you will be able to ensure the vehicle is consistently in optimal mechanical shape and fully charged. It will always be accessible for your use twenty-four hours a day, and there will be no need to search for an available rental e-scooter on the street that may not have much of a remaining charge. Owning your own e-scooter will **avoid the embedded tracking software encoded into most rental vehicles.** It is imperative that you are able to ride **"in the black"** free of surveillance or external tracking by some unknown adversary. Only by owning your own vehicle can you fully rely on it to be ready to whisk you to a safe location during a security incident or emergency.

BICYCLES

A bicycle is an excellent and efficient way to move quickly about a city. Prices vary significantly based on the style, quality, and features of a bicycle. Considering security, bikes have some advantages and disadvantages compared to other vehicles. One disadvantage is that they are much easier to steal than a car, truck, or most motorcycles. Thieves may be drawn to steal a flashy, high-end road bike that is outfitted with all of the latest technology due to its visual appeal and significant monetary value. Aggressive criminals may even be interested in stealing a bike by force at an intersection or wherever they can get their hands on a rider. If you are primarily commuting around a city and locking your bike in publicly accessible locations, it may be best to choose a modest model with a much lower value that is less enticing to thieves.

One advantage of riding a bike is that there is generally no need to charge it since most models are completely powered by the pedaling of the rider. Although **electric bicycles (e-bikes)** are available with an onboard battery to provide rider assistance or fully power a bike for a period of time, this eliminates the advantage of never requiring a charge. E-bikes are much heavier and may draw special attention from thieves when locked in an accessible location on the street. E-bikes have a significant speed advantage but require a greater investment and more attention than a standard bicycle. An e-bike, just like an e-scooter, is technically categorized as a "motorized micro-mobility device."

You may be able to store your bicycle inside a secure area or within your home or apartment, but if you are riding around a city, it is likely that you will have to lock your bike in a public setting much of the time. This is a disadvantage since it can be hard to effectively secure a bike. Criminals may steal the bike seat or one of the wheels, especially if the wheels have a quick-release feature. Even if the bike and both wheels are properly secured to an immovable object with a bike lock, there is still a substantial risk that a vandal could cut the tires,

damage the chain, or tamper with the bicycle in a way that it could fail while traveling at high speeds resulting in injury. When returning to your bike after locking it in a public location, always check for tampering to ensure that no parts have been removed and that the bike has not been damaged. A brief check may help avoid a dangerous crash a few moments later.

In some cities, enclosed bicycle lockers are available near major attractions or outside subway stations. Some bike lockers can be rented on an annual or monthly basis to ensure their availability when needed. They feature a fully enclosed storage space that provides secure protection from theft, tampering, and the effects of weather. This is a great solution if available and eliminates some of the security disadvantages of storing a bike.

WALKING AND RUNNING

Walking and running are key modes of transportation for many people, especially in the city and suburbs. This section will discuss some techniques to **MITIGATE RISK** while on foot and what to do if someone is following you.

When walking or running, be aware of your location on the sidewalk, especially wide city sidewalks. Always walk well away from any doorways that open onto the sidewalk. This includes all doorways such as stores, shops, homes, alleys, gates, etc. **Goal: position yourself on the sidewalk to avoid being surprised by an adversary lying in wait who grabs you and pulls you against your will inside a business or home or into a secluded area out of sight of others on the street.** Although more probable at night, this type of surprise attack can also happen during the day, depending on where you are walking or running. Pay close attention if you live in an area that experiences periods of limited visibility due to fog, sandstorms, smoke, or other environmental concerns since these conditions can also be exploited by an adversary.

Be careful about walking too close to the street curb. In some cities, there are endless cars parked next to the curb where someone can hide, surprising a victim as they pass by. In other cities, there are vast stretches of sidewalk where no parking is allowed along the curb. Be careful in these circumstances of walking too close to the street, especially if you are carrying a handbag or messenger bag slung over a shoulder on the street curbside.

STAY SAFE

Stay Safe When Walking with a Handbag

In one city, an attack technique has been reported that consists of two men on a scooter slowly riding up behind an unsuspecting victim walking on the sidewalk along the street near the curb. The victim generally has a handbag slung over her shoulder on the side closest to the street curb.

While the front attacker focuses on driving the scooter, the second attacker on the back of the bike employs a sharp knife with a long blade to slash the handbag strap of the unsuspecting woman. After violently slashing the handbag strap, the second attacker grabs the now-freed bag, and the scooter speeds away. The woman is left bleeding and injured on the sidewalk with a severe cut to her arm, and her handbag long gone. This can happen during both day and night.

You can potentially foil this attack technique and limit surprise by walking well away from the street curb with your handbag slung over your shoulder, which is furthest from the street. Stay aware at all times.

Considering these challenges, it is important to know where you are walking and what issues are most **PROBABLE** in your particular area. On a wide city street, walk with the flow of pedestrians, and if there are few people on the sidewalk, choose a path closer to the center of the sidewalk. Regardless of where you walk or run on the sidewalk, always keep your head up and your eyes focused on what is going on in the immediate vicinity. **It is imperative to keep your attention focused outward on the immediate environment and NOT on your mobile device. Do NOT block out your immediate environment by listening to loud music through headphones or earbuds. Save the entertainment for another time in a safe and secure space.** When out on the street, **YOU ARE EXPOSED**, and vigilance is important. As noted earlier in this book, it is your choice, but choices have ramifications.

When walking or running in a quiet area without other pedestrians or runners, such as on a running trail through the woods or alone in a quiet neighborhood, pay special attention to locations where you can quickly seek help if needed. While traveling on your route, mentally note places that you pass to where you could rapidly return for assistance. If you feel that a potential adversary is following in a vehicle, your goal is to move in a manner that is either difficult or impossible for a car or truck to follow. Motorcycles, scooters, and bicycles are all much more agile, and the riders will be more capable of following you through some of these techniques.

1) Reverse course.

If you feel that a car is shadowing behind you or someone is driving along the street next to you and perhaps has lowered their car window to try to talk with you, simply **reverse your direction 180 degrees and go back the way you came**. An automobile would be forced to turn around or drive in reverse to maintain contact with you; both of these actions are extremely alerting and demonstrate the clear intent of the driver to pursue you. Backtrack to a **HARD POINT** or another location that you identified along your route where you can seek help.

2) Go where no vehicle can go.

Jump a fence. Cut through a tree line. Cross a drainage ditch. Wade or swim across a stream. Travel on a narrow path that is too small for a vehicle to follow. Continuously maintain an awareness of areas where you can travel on foot and where no vehicle of any type can follow.

3) Use buildings with multiple entrances and exits.

Make it exceedingly difficult for an adversary to follow you by passing through structures with numerous entrances and exits.

An adversary cannot predict where you will exit and will be forced to either get out of their vehicle and follow on foot or risk losing you along the way. They will also have to stay quite close while inside the facility or risk losing sight of you; they will not be able to hang back and observe from a distance. This can help to "smoke out the adversary" and make them show their hand.

If you are near a large, multi-level business such as a shopping mall or an outlet mall, enter at one entrance, quickly switch levels, and then depart from a separate exit on a different level on the opposite side of the mall. It is extremely difficult for an adversary to continue to follow you unless they exit their vehicle and maneuver on foot.

This technique also works well with a large office building that has multiple entrances and exits. Keep in mind that the parking garage may also serve as another possible entrance or exit, further complicating an adversary's efforts to follow you. Choose an unpredictable route and exit through a separate portion of the building. Your adversary will quickly lose track of you. Disappear or move to a location where you can seek help.

4) Make a scene.

If you are unable to break contact and fully escape from an adversary, instead move quickly to a location where there are a lot of people. Scream at the top of your lungs, "Help!" and waive your arms to maximize the visual effect. Draw the attention of others who can promptly come to your aid. If it is nighttime, run toward a well-lit area so that others can see you and offer assistance; this will also remove some of the advantages that darkness may provide to an adversary. Be aware that the light will immediately destroy any limited night vision that you have already developed while outside in the darkness. Everything is a trade-off.

Carry a Security Whistle

Consider purchasing and carrying a **high-end security whistle,** which can help you draw a lot of attention and quickly get assistance. This specially designed whistle emits an extremely loud, shrill sound in excess of 120 dB from a small, indestructible metal tube, often made of titanium. Some models are so loud that they can be heard up to one mile away. With its special lightweight design, this type of high-efficiency whistle can be worn on a neck lanyard inside your shirt and is immediately available for use in an emergency. It is an affordable and effective tool for both adults and children and requires no training to use.

WATERCRAFT

Watercraft can be a great choice of transportation for those who live near a body of water, such as an ocean, a lake, or even a river. Some people use watercraft for work purposes, and others for pleasure or just to relax. The unique capabilities of watercraft also make them valuable for certain security

situations that you and your loved ones may face. These unique situations will be discussed in **Volume III, Part 1,** *Civil Unrest*. In this section, we offer some comments on a few types of watercraft worthy of further consideration in your overall security plan.

1) Traditional boats.

Depending on the size and type, traditional boats can offer significant capabilities for you and your loved ones if you need to depart from a troubled area for an extended period of time. Many models offer comfortable sleeping and dining facilities and can support a journey lasting either days or weeks, but at a significant price that may be well out of reach. If you live near the ocean or a major lake and have ample financial resources, a traditional boat may provide options should your security situation degrade.

2) Inflatable boats.

For some purposes, a smaller inflatable boat may be a great option. Boats in this class often add a small but muscular outboard engine that capably provides substantial power and speed due to the light weight of the boat. Inflatable boats are a fast, reliable means of transportation with a relatively small footprint. Although lacking many of the capabilities and features of larger traditional boats, inflatable boats may be a good choice for short trips based on your personal needs. They are much more affordable than fiberglass boats and can be deflated for easier transport and storage. If you and your loved ones are adventurous and physically fit, these boats can also operate on human power with paddles when stealth is desired, as demonstrated by some elite teams in the military and other organizations.

3) Personal watercraft (PWC).

These small jet-drive boats pack a lot of performance and features for a price that is more reasonable than purchasing a much larger boat. They offer extended range, high speeds, and agile performance for one or more passengers, depending on the model. Some law enforcement agencies that are responsible for sections of inland waterways or the coastline make frequent use of PWCs, which is a testament to their utility. PWCs provide excellent capabilities that can be fully exploited to assist with any security plan.

4) Canoes and kayaks.

Canoes and kayaks are silent, relatively fast, and have a very low footprint during both day and night. They require paddling (human power) to move, or they can drift with the current based on the body of water where they are employed. Paddling may be a limiting factor based on your level of endurance and physical fitness or the distance that needs to be covered. Both canoes and kayaks are lightweight and affordable and offer an excellent way to quickly depart from an area if trouble breaks out, especially on rivers.

ROAD RAGE

Road rage has become an unfortunate reality in many places around the United States. One driver's actions can push another driver over the edge, and an irritating situation can quickly turn into a violent and possibly deadly encounter. Traveling to and from work may be one of the most dangerous times for you and your loved ones due to the number of road rage incidents. This topic warrants some thought and planning to effectively **MITIGATE RISK**.

What does road rage look like? It can take many forms, but a few scenarios follow to show the variety and craziness of human behavior on the highways. Pay close attention to the "What to Do, What Not to Do" section after each scenario to learn how to effectively manage road rage should you find yourself in a similar situation.

WHAT TO DO, WHAT NOT TO DO

Bumper Cars

One early weekday morning on a neighborhood road in Northern Virginia heading toward Washington, D.C., two men driving large SUVs became irritated with one another. The situation escalated quickly, with both drivers leapfrogging past each other on a narrow road, jockeying for position. Their speeds continued to increase along the road, putting others in the vicinity of their childish antics at great risk. As the situation boiled over, the two SUVs continued side-by-side down the two-lane road, scraping their doors and repeatedly banging into one another as one driver attempted to push the other off the suburban neighborhood road into a deep drainage ditch. Police were contacted via 9-1-1 by a bystander and responded in short order. Both drivers were fully engaged in the jousting match, and neither would relent.

WHAT TO DO, WHAT NOT TO DO:

The situation was surreal, considering the quiet neighborhood road that served as the backdrop for this vehicular altercation. It shows that road rage can happen quickly to anyone and spiral completely out of control. The two drivers were so involved in their jousting as they drove side-by-side down the two-lane road that they did not appear to appreciate they were blocking any on-coming traffic. This could have easily resulted in a catastrophic head-on collision ending with fatalities. Both sides of the road had deep drainage ditches that would have caused any vehicle that went off the road to come to an immediate and abrupt stop, likely resulting in extreme injury or death.

Either participant would have been much smarter to de-escalate the situation before it became a car-on-car attack. If you find yourself in this type of situation, **reduce speed and disengage from the altercation, but do not stop moving.** Keep your vehicle rolling and look for an avenue to get away from your adversary. In this situation, there were numerous side streets on both sides of the road that could have served as an "off-ramp" and allowed either of the drivers to exit the scene and **BREAK CONTACT**. If one of the drivers had simply pulled over and stopped, the other driver could have pulled up alongside at close range or exited their vehicle to engage further on a face-to-face basis. The situation would have entered a new phase that could have proven just as dangerous. By continuing to move, even if slowly, there is no opportunity for one of the drivers to exit their vehicle and engage at close range.

This was a scenario where both drivers were competitive and wanted to establish their dominance over the other driver. Be the smarter driver and let the other person push on ahead and "win" the engagement. Take a deep breath, de-escalate, and escape from the situation.

WHAT TO DO, WHAT NOT TO DO

The Make-Up Artist

Sometimes, road rage can happen even when traffic is stuck at a standstill. On a major secondary road heading into the city, the early morning rush hour traffic was backed up, and all cars were at a complete stop. One driver decided to maximize her time in the traffic jam and focused all of her attention on applying her make-up in the interior rearview mirror of her large SUV. Unfortunately, she did not immediately recognize that she had stopped her vehicle on an incline in this section of the road. Engrossed in her make-up application, the woman's SUV started to roll backward.

The driver immediately behind the woman had intentionally maintained several feet of distance between the SUV and the front of his expensive sedan. He was quietly gazing ahead at the stationary traffic when he noticed the woman's vehicle begin to roll backward. The man hit his horn to alert the driver in front that her SUV was rolling backward but to no avail. He hit his horn again and then again. BOOM. The large SUV hit the man's car. The woman turned her head around, shocked at the impact. She had been oblivious to the movement of her SUV.

The man exited his now-damaged car, walked up to the woman's SUV, and beat on her window to get her attention while yelling at her. She was terrified and confused about what had just transpired. One moment, she is putting on make-up and listening to her car stereo, and seconds later, she is in an accident and facing an angry stranger beating on her window. There was nowhere for her to go since traffic was stopped in all directions. Nearby drivers looked on with morbid curiosity, but no one had any inclination to intervene on the woman's behalf or get involved in the developing situation. The man, although furious, took a deep breath and walked back to his car to call the authorities and report the accident.

WHAT TO DO, WHAT NOT TO DO:

Fortunately, this situation quickly calmed down, but it could have just as easily taken a much more difficult and unfortunate path. This accident was completely avoidable, and that was likely the cause of the man's rage. The woman in this scenario was distracted by her make-up application, which led to the accident. Many instances of road rage are caused by distracted driving, whether the vehicle is moving or stationary. **To avoid a major cause of road rage, focus on driving when behind the wheel.** Do not text. Do not check social media feeds. Do not talk endlessly on the phone, letting your mind drift off into the depths of the conversation as if you were located 1000 miles away. Even while waiting at traffic lights, avoid these behaviors. Free your car of distractions while you drive. Do not forget that your primary responsibility while driving is to safely operate the vehicle. **By taking these steps and focusing just on driving, the likelihood of involvement in a road rage situation is significantly lessened. MITIGATE RISK.**

It is important to consider a few other points about this situation. The woman in the SUV did one thing correctly: **she kept her vehicle's doors locked**. This simple step maintained a limited barrier between her and the angry driver from the other car. The locked doors prevented the man from having an easy opportunity to gain access to the interior of the woman's SUV and allowed him a few extra moments to cool off and walk away from the situation. Could he have broken the SUV's window to unlock the car door and gain direct access to the woman? Sure, it is **POSSIBLE**, but that would be a significant escalation in this situation, and the locked door may have been just enough to allow the situation to calm down. Also, keep in mind that unless you have an armored vehicle with bullet-resistant glass, cars do not stop bullets.

What if the man continued to seek entry to the SUV and the incident worsened? The woman would have to **GET OFF THE X** as quickly as possible before the man could lay his hands on her or engage her with a weapon through the window or the soft metal skin of the vehicle. Sheet metal may feel tough to a human hand but not to bullets. One option

for the woman is to quickly exit the vehicle through the passenger side door, keeping the SUV between her and the irate
man. Remain behind **COVER,** such as the engine block or one
of the wheels, to the greatest extent possible while maintaining positive visual contact with your adversary. Do not
lose sight of your adversary. At this point, consider running
from the scene to a position of increased safety, which may
be well off the road, away from the SUV and the altercation.
This is especially true if your adversary brandishes a weapon,
and you are unarmed; it is time to go—NOW. It is possible
that a bystander may provide assistance once the situation
significantly worsens, but this cannot be relied on. Run away
and retrieve your vehicle later after the situation has been
resolved. If the situation degrades further and you stay with
your vehicle, you may not need it anymore.

Another option is to stay and fight. **IT DEPENDS.** In some
states, your vehicle is considered an extension of your home.
If the man attempted to enter the SUV or pull the woman
out of the vehicle, it may be considered a **LETHAL THREAT
situation, and LETHAL FORCE may be justified to control
the threat**. This depends on the laws of the state where the
incident occurs. It is your responsibility to learn the laws in
advance so you know with certainty what you legally can and
cannot do to defend yourself and your loved ones.

WHAT TO DO, WHAT NOT TO DO

Reckless Disregard

A young woman was running errands after work in an
upscale suburb of a major East Coast city. Sitting in her car at
a busy traffic signal, the young woman was first in line and
waiting for the long red light to turn green. She was rapidly

texting with one of her friends, unaware that the light had changed, and it was now her turn to go. Several seconds passed, but she remained focused on her texting, and her car was still stationary. The driver behind her honked his car's horn once to encourage her to move. Startled and irritated by the honking, the woman immediately gave the proverbial "one-finger salute" to the other driver and sped away in her luxury sedan, figuring that was the end of the situation. She was wrong.

The man driving the other vehicle was furious at the gesture and was not going to let the woman in the fancy car get away with it. He accelerated rapidly and chased after her. He saw that her car had a custom vanity license plate that displayed the name and seal of the prestigious university from which the woman had graduated a few years earlier.

The woman quickly observed the man's car taking chase, and she turned off the main road into a quiet neighborhood at the first opportunity. She accelerated her powerful car to high speeds through the winding streets, going faster and faster until her car was traveling at over seventy miles per hour in a twenty-five mile per hour residential zone. Although her lead had increased, she could see that the man was still following in his car. The woman sped through a stop sign without stopping or even slowing down, putting others in the neighborhood at great risk while focusing on her flight from the angry man. The man continued to pursue fervently and would not relent.

Entering a sharp curve, the woman slammed on her brakes and felt the thumping of her car's anti-lock braking system (ABS) as it worked to dump the energy and lower the speed of her car. The ABS prevented the brakes from locking up and causing a loss of control. She observed in her rearview mirror that the man was now gaining ground and closing the gap between their two cars.

Speeding through yet another neighborhood with reckless abandon and no regard for the safety of others, the woman skidded around a sharp curve, narrowly avoiding two large trash containers in the street in front of one of the homes. Looking straight ahead, she saw a long stretch of railroad tracks in the distance and yelled, "Yes! Finally!" She figured she could rapidly accelerate and get away from her pursuer. Her heart was racing as she observed the gate barrier arms begin to lower. A train was rapidly approaching and began to blow its horn as it neared the intersection. She thought, "I will lose this guy here when I get over the tracks!" She slammed the accelerator pedal to the floor, racing through the inter-section over the tracks. BAM!!! She clipped one of the wooden barrier arms as it was lowering, breaking the wooden arm into several pieces. The woman was through the intersection. Within a few seconds, the extended train rolled through the intersection, completely blocking her adversary from further pursuit—this time.

Shaking with the adrenaline pulsing through her body, the woman guided her vehicle into another neighborhood to get off the road and change direction. She drove into an empty elementary school parking lot adjacent to the road and shut off her car. The woman felt sick to her stomach (likely due to the overload of adrenaline), and she was confused. She thought, "What just happened? What was his problem? What a jerk!" A thousand thoughts rushed through her mind as she sat alone in the parking lot. She got out of her vehicle and noticed the deep, long scrape on her car's roof where the wooden barrier arm had hit. She was furious and scared. Shak-ing it off, she got back into her car and carefully made her way through back streets toward her condominium across town. She did not see the man again and soon arrived at home.

WHAT TO DO, WHAT NOT TO DO:

There are several valuable lessons to be learned from this scenario.

1) Be courteous on the road; no situation warrants the "one-finger salute." Countless news reports over the years have shown that this gesture can amplify a point of friction or turn a simple misunderstanding into a real problem, sometimes with catastrophic or even fatal results. This gesture is truly offensive throughout the United States and in several countries around the world and will usually receive a strong response. **AVOID, AVOID, AVOID.**

After hearing the other driver's car horn, it would have been preferable for the woman to simply resume driving through the intersection and internally recognize that she was not paying attention when the light turned green. No further response was necessary toward the other driver. Self-reflect and improve for next time.

2) You often do not know with whom you are dealing in this type of confrontation. What is going through your adversary's head? You are not dealing with their mood only at this moment. Did the other person have an argument with their significant other an hour ago? Is this person going through a tough divorce? Is he late to work? Is he drunk or on drugs? Is your adversary suffering from anger management issues and is totally out of control? Is the person a violent criminal? Without knowing the individual, you have no idea what is going on in their life just prior to this incident. Your gesture may be the final thing that sets the person off.

3) Everyone is a "tough guy" while they are in their vehicle. This is common street wisdom in some parts of the country, especially in the Northeast. People will often do or say things from the perceived security of their vehicle that may lead to disastrous personal results once they are forced to get out of their car. To **MITIGATE RISK** and be a good neighbor, remember two pieces of well-known advice: **"Do not write checks that your body cannot cash," and "Treat others the way you want to be treated yourself."**

4) Vanity plates clearly identify your vehicle. As mentioned earlier, vanity plates make it easier for an adversary to identify your car when following you. These plates also increase the likelihood of an adversary recognizing your car at a later point around town. The person may still harbor ill feelings toward you about the incident and could even want to cause trouble days or weeks later if they see you again. **LIVE UNDER THE RADAR.**

5) Excessive speed will end poorly. The woman in this scenario kept going faster and faster, hoping to escape from her adversary through sheer speed. This dramatically increased her risk of having a significant car accident through loss of control or hitting a pedestrian somewhere along her route. What if a child ran out into the road after a ball or someone was walking their dog in the street? The woman would have been challenged to rapidly avoid a collision which may have resulted in the death of an innocent victim.

Do not bring about your own demise through poor judgment. Instead, drive smoothly and safely at a controlled speed to a nearby **HARD POINT,** such as a police precinct. Do not stop or exit your vehicle until you have reached safety. Keep your car moving.

6) Distracted driving causes issues. We have hammered this topic home throughout this chapter. Focus on the task at hand: **DRIVING**. Save the other activities for later.

GLOSSARY

The definitions below apply to our purposes throughout this book.

Adversary: Depending on your specific personal situation, life circumstances, employment, or where you are located in the world, this may be an individual or group that has a different interest set than you or your loved ones. It may consist of enemies, criminals, hackers, or even an authoritarian government abroad.

Area knowledge: For our purposes, area knowledge consists of learning important details about a city and the surrounding suburbs where you and your loved ones live, work, study, and play.

Avoid, avoid, avoid: Proactively look for potential problems and mitigate the risk by making alternate choices and avoiding the issue altogether. Plan now to avoid problems later. No one can defend against all threats, but excellent preparation can help avoid many.

Baseline: Routine, standard patterns of behavior or events that are regularly associated with a specific person, environment, or situation. When something deviates from these norms or seems out of place, it may warrant further investigation.

Break contact: Putting distance between you and the aggressor by running or driving away.

Chaining: A technique where people move together through a chaotic situation by linking arms to prevent getting separated.

Concealment: Protection from observation. Concealment provides no protection from the effects of firearms or explosives. ("She used the bushes in the park as **concealment** so that the gang members would not see her and would just keep walking along the bike path toward the subway station.")

Cover: Protection from the effects of firearms or explosives. ("Once the rifleman started shooting, the police officer yelled out for everyone to quickly take **cover** to protect them from the incoming bullets.")

Demeanor hit: By closely observing a person's collective behavior or actions in a situation, an intuitive, educated guess can be made about their true activity or intentions. For example, you may be extremely confident that a person is following you or watching you based on the way they act (a demeanor hit) when you move through a portion of your route. The person may hurry to catch up so they do not lose sight of you while moving through a building or along a winding street, or they may simply pay too much attention to your activities under a certain set of circumstances. With experience, the ability to correctly identify demeanor hits increases.

Find, fix, and finish: A process used to locate the enemy (FIND), confirm the location and pattern of life (FIX), and then take action against the target (FINISH). Criminals often use a similar thought process to FIND their targets (potential

victims), figure out how and where they can get to the targets (FIX), and then commit their crimes at the place of their
choosing (FINISH).

Getting off the X: The "X" is a location where something bad
happens, such as an assault, robbery, attempted kidnapping, or
another type of crime. An adversary often plans their activities
in advance and chooses a place that is advantageous for their
goals and under their control. When something bad happens,
your immediate goal is to get out of this area, eliminate the
adversary's advantage, and move away as quickly as possible.

Hard point: A location that provides a degree of protection
by limiting direct observation and providing physical separation so that an adversary is either incapable of pursuit or the
environment is deemed too risky for their goals or activities.
Examples may include homes, workplaces, places of worship,
hospitals, government buildings, or a sizable commercial
establishment with a lot of people onsite.

Improvised explosive device (IED): A homemade bomb or
destructive device produced in an unlimited variety of form
factors limited only by the imagination and creativity of the
bombmaker. Consists of some type of explosive, a detonat-
ing mechanism, and often items to produce fragmentation
wounds, such as nails, screws, or glass which generate shrap-
nel following an explosion. These devices can be either simple
or complex based on the skill of the bombmaker.

In the Black: The state of being completely free of any physical
or technical surveillance, external tracking, or monitoring of
any type by an adversary or some unknown entity. ("He slipped
away into the evening on his e-scooter, leaving his electronics

behind. After numerous turns through the city, he knew he was **in the Black.**")

KISS Principle: "Keep It Simple Stupid." Although blunt, this advice is timeless and sound in its logic. It is especially important to apply this principle when conducting planning. If a plan or activity seems too complicated or has too many moving parts, refer back to this principle and make adjustments.

Lethal threat: A threat of grievous body harm or death. Although the legal specifics may vary among jurisdictions, when faced with a lethal threat and in fear for their life, a person has the right to apply **deadly force** (also known as **lethal force**) to protect themselves and **control the threat.** Each person is responsible for learning the laws in advance and knowing with certainty what is legally justified in a specific jurisdiction.

Mitigating risk: Making wise choices to manage the level of risk associated with a particular event or sequence of events. Everything in life has some degree of risk, whether it is high, medium, or low. Sometimes, several small decisions made in sequence may add up to an unacceptably high level of risk when combined, resulting in a catastrophic failure.

Pattern of life: The collection of human patterns that make up a person's life, including when and where they eat, work, study, sleep, take breaks, spend time with family or friends, worship, shop, use the restroom, etc. Over time, many human behaviors will fall into patterns that can be identified and exploited by an adversary.

Personal space: A safety buffer extending approximately three feet from your body in all directions. Allowing others into this personal space eliminates the ability to react quickly to a threat. The concept of acceptable personal space varies somewhat among cultures.

Possible versus Probable: Consider what is **possible** in a particular situation and then evaluate what is **probable**. In a world of limited time and resources, focus efforts on defending against the **probable**. It is not viable to react to everything (the **possible**); otherwise, you will always be reacting.

Printing: A term that describes when the outline of a concealed firearm or weapon is visible through the clothing that covers it, potentially alerting others to the presence of a concealed weapon. Printing should be avoided to maintain a tactical advantage and ensure that others are unaware of the presence of a weapon.

Standard operating procedure (SOP): A systematic, standardized way of performing a task that ensures thoroughness and efficiency. Well-developed and practiced SOPs may lead to greater speed of execution under stressful conditions.

Targeting: The collection and identification of detailed information or insights about a specific person or entity to enable further pursuit or exploitation in support of an adversary's goals. The subject of the targeting process is referred to as a **target**. Targeting can range in complexity from the abbreviated process used by a common street criminal committing a mugging or burglary to the strategic process used by a state actor while pursuing a wanted international terrorist or an entire terrorist organization operating in numerous countries across the globe.

ABOUT THE AUTHOR

 **TIM BEARD** has over three decades of experience in the public and private sectors. He served on active duty in the **U.S. Marine Corps** as an infantry officer, attaining the grade of captain. Tim served in various command and staff positions at the battalion, company, and platoon levels, including two separate company commands. Additionally, he was selected as the Aide-de-Camp for a Two-Star Marine Corps commanding general. While assigned to the Fleet Marine Force (FMF), Tim deployed to seventeen countries in Europe, Latin America, and Africa.

Tim was recruited by the **Central Intelligence Agency (CIA)** into the Directorate of Operations (Clandestine Service). After completing arduous training as an operations officer, Tim conducted and managed extremely sensitive clandestine operations around the globe for the U.S. Government, including overseas postings to multiple countries in Asia and the Middle East. Over the course of his CIA career, Tim developed deep expertise in sophisticated intelligence operations, covert action, counterterrorism, counterintelligence, cybersecurity, risk assessment and mitigation, crisis management, and working in high-threat environments.

After retiring from CIA, Tim founded a global intelligence

and risk mitigation consulting company, assisting clients in achieving strategic and tactical objectives in high-pressure environments under complex circumstances. He has helped clients to create a competitive advantage by driving decision-making and facilitating business opportunities.

Over the course of his life, Tim has lived in ten states in diverse regions across the United States. This varied background has provided a broad and unique understanding of the cultures and values that exist across this vast nation. Tim has honed his everyday security skills through his extensive life experiences in the United States and while living and working abroad in advanced and developing nations, as well as extremely dangerous war zones. In addition to living in numerous locales, Tim has traveled broadly in the United States and overseas.

Tim earned a Master of International Policy and Practice from the Elliott School of International Affairs at the George Washington University. He also holds a Bachelor of Arts in Political Science from Auburn University.

COMING SOON:

Look Twice: Your Guide to Staying Safe with Tech,

Travel, and Natural Disasters

VOLUME II